DATABASE DESIGN MADE EASY

Effective relational database design for ordinary people

M. CLINTON JONES

Diogenes
Academic
Press

Legal information

Database Design Made Easy: Effective Relational Database Design for Ordinary People
M. Clinton Jones

This edition published 2014 by Diogenes Academic Press

Diogenes Academic Press is an imprint of Bristol Folk Publications
www.bristol–folk.co.uk

ISBN 13: 978–1–909953–55–0

Digital layout and realisation by Diogenes Academic Press

CONTENTS

About the author

It was a rubber–keyed Spectrum that introduced M. Clinton Jones to IT. He bought said computer in the mid–1980s to document his then sprawling progressive jazz, folk and rock vinyl record collection. He discovered quickly what 48K meant; he only got as far as *Can* before the Spectrum started randomly transposing characters because it couldn't cope with the sheer volume of data. It went back in the box.

In 1994 he tried his hand with IT again and left behind the drudgery of the NHS (eleven years of mopping blood from operating theatre floors) to enrol on an introductory computing course. He progressed by slow turns to getting that degree he'd always promised himself – First Class with Honours, no less – which led to a teaching job at his old university, though, if truth be known he was already teaching there even before he got his degree. Many years later he now teaches database development (amongst other things) at the University of Bristol.

His first foray into print was in *The Rough Guide to Rock*, 3rd edition (Penguin/Rough Guides) in 1998, whilst back in academia he co–wrote several journal papers and a conference paper. He is vaguely annoyed that his academic contributions all appear as *et al* in most popular referencing styles. Other highlights include contributing to a Government White Paper on the IT Infrastructure Library (ITIL) and writing for various magazines and journals on subjects as diverse as music and railways.

In 2009 his first book, *Bristol Folk*, was published. *The Guardian* and the *English Folk Dance and Song Society* (and many others) said nice things about it. Subsequent books on various aspects of music (and railway sound recording) history all received excellent reviews and one, *The B&C Discography*, was recently nominated for an international excellence in musical history award. At time of going to press he has no idea if his book is amongst the winners. He'll know in September 2014.

He doesn't talk about his, so far, one–off detour into children's fiction, not that he used his real name for that one. Not that it is really for children either. There might be a second volume.

Meanwhile, the 20th anniversary of his introduction to databases seems a fitting time to present his own contribution to database design. And here it is.

FOREWORD

This book debags the myth that designing relational databases is *difficult*. Nothing could be further from the truth – that is once you drop all the unnecessary baggage of relational theory. The secret is that you don't need to know anything about the theory to design relational databases.

And that's where relational database writers go wrong every time. They all seem to think that relational theory is something that the normal person in the street needs to *understand* before they can build their database – and the immediate assumption is that you really want to know about every small nuance behind the esoteric beast that is relational theory. This can take anything up to 400 pages. Perhaps more.

What doesn't seem to cross the writer's mind is that you probably want a database *right now, today* to do something or other specific, be that to support your research, exploit a business opportunity or make sense of your sprawling sci–fi book collection. It never occurs to them that you don't want to have your time wasted on reams of stuff that adds no value for you.

The reality is that most people with a pressing need to build a database haven't got the slightest interest in learning all about (never mind *understanding*) 3rd normal form, referential integrity constraints, schema depictions or denormalisation.

Which is why I wrote this book. It's here to fill a very large gap in a generally unsatisfied market, which is for people that need to design a small–scale, one–off database *right now, today*.

Database Design Made Easy is the book I wish I'd had twenty years ago. With this book in your hand, you can just get on with the immediate task of designing your database in an intuitive way. With crayons, if you like. You'll still have to do a spot of thinking, but it's the sort that can be done gently over a nice cup of tea and a bun. Job done.

Thanks to:

My wife, Janette, for putting up with it all; the deterioration of the Tunisian weather for giving me the perfect excuse to finally sit down in my hotel room and write the first full draft of the book – even though the holiday was booked for the express purpose of doing this, not much got done until the storms started; Maggie Kneller for proofreading, making sensible suggestions as to which bits to discard (i.e. most of the bits that I thought were funny) and for testing the technique (just one more time never hurts); relational theory for being possibly the only subject area about which there are no *funny* jokes, not even the one about going up to two tables in a bar and asking if you can join them.

INTRODUCTION

The traditional approach to relational database design involves an uneasy marriage of art and science because of all the *guesswork* that tends to go alongside the more formalised techniques, thus making the subject rather more difficult than those where you just have to follow a simple and prescribed set of steps through from a to z to get a reasonable result.

It could be viewed as amusing, in that case, that this book concentrates on the *artistic* to do away with the need for the *scientific*. In so doing it provides a simple and prescribed set of steps to follow, from which you will get that reasonable result that you're looking for. It has taken decades, I know, but finally relational theory has been made simple. Well, ignored, to be honest.

What this book does is tell you to get drawing – and you can use as many different colours as you like. What's that? You're not artistic? Well, it doesn't matter – as long as you can draw different sized rectangles and straightish lines, then you'll get on just fine. Colouring in is optional.

If this doesn't make the book – and the technique covered within – revolutionary, then I don't know what does. And the lovely thing is that this short book, in intending to do one thing, instead does two things:

> **1.** It lets anyone design relational databases. This was intentional.
> **2.** By concentrating on how you want your database to look and act from the perspective of using it, it also provides you with a blueprint for a database that will be easy to use. This was a happy accident, though inevitable, when you think about it.

To illustrate the simple steps of the TONTO Technique© the book presents three typical scenarios where a relational database represents a sensible solution. It then pulls you gently through the steps to come out at the other end with, not just your relational design, but also the aforementioned blueprint with which you can move straight on to building your database.

Why is it called the TONTO Technique©?

Although I've used the technique presented in this book since the late 1990s, I've had quite a few problems working out how to best present something in book form that I had long since 'internalised'. Hence stopping and starting on this book a silly number of times over a ten year period.

As at early 2014 there was one very big sticking point, which was that all of my attempts to describe the simple tasks involved in my design method sounded too technical and difficult – not good attributes for a book that was trying to make things easy for people. The *aha!* moment of simplicity arrived whilst I was listening to Tonto's second and final album, *About Time*, in Tunisia in March 2014.

The sticking point was that I was trying to cross–reference my method with relational design so as to make clear that my approach, though unconventional, does things in a rigorous enough way to count as a bona fide relational design method. The *aha!* moment told me to ignore relational theory altogether; that in terms of my method it was an irrelevance. My method does the job without recourse to the traditional relational design methods, so why worry about them? Why does it take a holiday to realise the very, very obvious?

So I named the technique after the band to which I was listening when the truth hit. As you do.

Tonto, for those that don't know, made wonderful music using an early modular Moog Series III synthesiser. The name stood for *The Original New Timbral Orchestra*. Oh yes, although the second album was credited just to *Tonto*, the first was credited to *Tonto's Expanding Head Band*. It was that sort of era.

Never heard of Tonto? Well, that might not have stopped you from listening to them without knowing. If you've heard Stevie Wonder's *Innervisions*, *Talking Book* or *Music In My Mind*, then you've been listening to Tonto. Steve Hillage's *Motivation Radio*, ditto. At least one Billy Preston LP and several Isley Brothers records, ditto. Others too, I would imagine.

I like the fact that *tonto* is also the Spanish word for *stupid*.

IS THIS BOOK FOR ME?

If you can visualise your data in terms of choosing it from drop–downs and typing it into lists, then you should have little or no trouble using this book. Drop–downs should be fairly self–explanatory, in that you choose your data from a set of options, but if you're not quite sure what I mean by lists (these are known as sub–forms), some typical data entry screen examples are included for your perusal. Basically, however, if you've used a spread sheet package like Microsoft Excel or created a table in Microsoft Word, then you have been working with lists of data. If you can't visualise your data in this way by the end of the book, then, to be honest, you probably shouldn't be working with data!

If you still haven't made up your mind, then the following provides an idea of what the book does and doesn't do, along with information on the intended audience.

What this book does

This book shows you how to design a relational database, simply and easily. The paper–based design you produce can then be converted easily into a working, fully–relational database using software, such as Microsoft Access 2013. *Getting the paper–based design right is 99% of the job*; from there, building the real thing is simple. Or, at least, it should be if you''ve got your relational design right. But that's what this book is here for.

Along the way, this book also blows apart the myth, long–asserted by well–paid relational database designers, that no one but said well–paid relational database designers can design relational databases properly. This is no longer true, I'm afraid.

What this book does not do

It does not blind you with impenetrable jargon and take over 400 pages in which to do it, neither does it force you to learn lots of esoteric theory that, in all probability, you'll never need to use again. If you know what you want a relational database for and can draw a simple data entry screen on paper, then you are capable of designing your database correctly using the TONTO Technique©.

Who this book is for

This book is for anyone who has a one–off need to design a small–scale, relational database. Worked examples are used for the following typical users:

- Collectors, such as those who want to keep track of their collection.
- Researchers, such as those needing to store their research data in such a way so as to assure data integrity and validity of datasets used in analysis.
- Small business owners, such as those who need to keep track of customers, sales and so on.

If your specific need isn't covered above – for example, if you are enrolled on an information systems or business analysis course, or indeed any other course, degree or otherwise, that includes relational database design – the method is so simple that the above examples will be sufficient to explain the TONTO Technique©, which is transferrable to any *sane* need for a small–scale relational database.

The same goes if you have just found yourself in the wonderful world of work and are suddenly expected to come up with a relational database design based on having admitted at the interview that you, "...know something about computers."

Who this book is not for

This book is not really intended for anyone who is already well–acquainted (and happy) with relational theory or whose job is to build large–scale, corporate databases. If you're designing large–scale, corporate databases, the assumption is that you already know what you're doing.

On the other hand, it never does to assume anything. Perhaps this book *is* for you before anyone finds out that you never did quite get the hang of relational design, but are just very convincing at interviews. Besides, the technique is scaleable – it just gets a tad more confusing the more data entry screens you need.

Thinking about it, the TONTO Technique© makes you think in terms of how end–users will use the database, so if you've never thought about your end–users before it will do you no harm to flick through this book. Corporate databases are generally used by non–techies so if this book helps you to design databases that normal people find easy to use, by concentrating first on the design of the data entry screens, then it's no bad thing.

Why doesn't this book tell me how to build my database?

There are several reasons why coming up with the relational design and the building of the subsequent database are split up into two separate books.

1. The design and development sides are traditionally divorced from each other both in reality and in print. Books either cover relational design or they cover the development side, not both. The two are very different things.
2. The above is because relational design is completely independent of whatever software you use to build the database. The upshot of that is that I don't know which relational database software you're going to use to build your database (though I can make a good guess, which is why I've based the second book around Microsoft Access 2013).
3. Mention of a specific software package on the book jacket could deter potential buyers who might think that the book would only be of use if they were users of said named software, which is not the case. As it says above, relational design is not tied to specific software.
4. Those who already use database software but don't necessarily know how to design databases (and there are a lot of them about) don't have to pay twice the amount for a book of which half will be of no use.
5. I don't want to have to rewrite this book every time a new version of Microsoft Access appears. Tarting up old books with 'funky', new jacket and interior designs is not something that I relish doing every year or so.

One last thing; are there any hidden assumptions?

The only assumption is that you know what you want a database for. The reasoning behind the assumption is hopefully not unreasonable, after all:

- If you are a researcher, you presumably know what data you need to collect to achieve the objectives of your research (if not, then go and have a serious talk with your academic supervisor immediately).
- If you are in business then you are likely, if you have reached the point of guessing that you need a database, to know what the problem or opportunity is that you want a database to either solve or exploit.
- If you are a collector, you will probably know exactly what you want a database to do to support your hobby – collectors seem to take to databases because collections and databases just go together.

BACKGROUND

Those impatient to get on with designing their database can ignore this and the following section if they want. If you're one of those wanting to cut to the chase, then start with the *Basics* section if you're new to databases, whilst those who are happy that they know what a database is (or simply don't care) can skip that section and go directly to *Essentials*, which, as the title suggests, contains information that you really need to know prior to moving on to the worked examples.

Why are books on relational design so difficult to understand?

It's just one of those things. I've tried various books over the years that claimed to make relational design easy. My first thought is that most fail in this stated intent.

However, the first problem is that not too many books tackle relational design head on. For example, books that tell you how to *build* databases quite sensibly tend to ignore the hitherto difficult design part. They generally just show you the features of whichever software package they cover and assume that you somehow, magically perhaps, already have your relational design hidden about your person, unlikely though this is.

Of those books that do tackle relational design, the biggest issue, from my point of view, is that most, if not all, assume that you have the overarching desire to *understand* relational theory. Admittedly, these tend to be written specifically as text books for those on courses where the understanding of relational theory is not an option, so the approach is understandable. But do most of them have to make the subject so inpenetrable along the way?

It's not all doom and gloom, however, and for those that want to discover the niceties of relational design (as opposed to using my method to ignore it), I can heartily recommend Carol Britton and Jill Doake's *Software System Development: A Gentle Introduction* for doing exactly what it says in the title (though bear in mind that their book covers a lot more ground than just relational design).

Otherwise, what the traditional approach tends to do is to give first year computing students panic attacks because many never get beyond page 20, never mind the other 380 or so pages. Page 20 is generally about half way through Chapter 1 and is often the point at which the terms *schema*, *referential integrity constraints* and *overlap preservation* are introduced (unless these appear in the introduction).

In this respect, this current book proves that less is definitely more. For a start this book is relatively short but, more importantly, it let's you in on a big secret, which is that you don't need to understand relational theory to design relational databases. Therefore, it doesn't waste your time on the subject. And unlike other books on the subject it doesn't take itself too seriously. The subject may be serious, but being all po–faced about it doesn't help to get your database designed, does it?

Before anyone jumps down my throat, I'm not trying to suggest that relational theory is useless – no, far from it; without relational theory we wouldn't have relational databases. When all is said and done, the whole point of this book is to show you how to come up with a relational design because you need a workable relational design from which to build a relational database. This book just doesn't use relational theory to do it, that's all.

Meanwhile, to get back to the question of why relational theory is so hard to get to grips with, I suppose that the trouble is that no–one seems to be able to describe the activities involved in relational database design in any way that makes sense to a non–technical audience. Myself included. The Britton and Doake book still comes closest of all those I've seen, but even this is deliberately geared at a technically–minded audience.

Pondering over the difficulty of presenting relational design to any audience, whether technically–literate or not, strongly suggests that everyone learns relational design the same way. At root, relational database design experts tend to teach the subject in the same way that they were taught it. Shades here of *if it ain't broke, then don't mend it*. But my argument is that it is broke, otherwise it wouldn't remain such an inpenetrable subject, even to many of those on database–related courses.

What those doing the teaching probably forget is that, out of how ever many people there were in their university or college class, they were probably amongst a very small minority to whom any of it ever made the slightest bit of sense. Does that mean that everyone else was sadly lacking or does it suggest that the method of teaching relational design needs a good looking at?

What no one appears to have done in the last forty or so years is to have taken a step back to ask if there is a better way to approach the teaching side of relational design – or, better still, to ask themselves if there is a way to come up with the same end result but without resorting to complex relational theory.

Except me, that is – and the sad thing is that it took me five or so years to come to terms with the fact that my extremely simple way of doing things actually worked. That and another ten years of inactivity before I bothered to tell anyone.

But, hang on a second, if the technique I've come up with is so simple, then surely someone else must have discovered it as well? Perhaps they have; there may be other self–taught, relational database designers out there who already do things my way. I just don't know.

Margaret Boden, in her book, *The Creative Mind: Myths and Mechanisms*, posits that there are two types of creativity, p–creativity and h–creativity. P–creativity, or psychological creativity, means an idea that is novel to the person having the idea, in that they haven't come across the idea elsewhere, but that it has already been thought of by others. H–creativity, or historical creativity, on the other hand, descibes an idea that has never been thought of before.

My issue with this is that I don't think that you can call any idea h–creative because there is no way of knowing whether or not the idea has been thought of before. The best that can be said is that it is possible that it is a completely novel idea but, equally, it may be one that has been thought of previously. If this is the case, then it was either not documented or the documentation has not yet come to light.

So, in the above terms, although I'm happy to go along for the moment with stating that my technique is the product of an h–creative idea, it is easily possible that others have had the same idea but have just not bothered to document it. After all, when the idea hit me, it seemed so obvious that my thoughts went along the lines of *if there was anything in it, then someone else would have written about it already*. So I didn't bother writing about it either.

Meanwhile, Boden's book goes on to state that the idea in itself is not enough, but it's what you do with the idea that counts. Which is where I fell down heavily. Sixteen years is a very long time to keep an idea to myself. The main reason for this was that, until recently, I thought that I must just have missed something very obvious; otherwise everyone would teach – and do – relational database design my way. By degrees, I realised that everyone else has missed something very obvious, not me.

What I'd done all those years ago was to take something complex, turn it on its head and come up with something simple. All it took was to look at the problem from the opposite direction; meaning from the direction of the database user, not the database designer.

So my idea was to start at the other end and ask those wanting databases to design how they wanted to enter their data in their data entry screen. What no one seems to have worked out is that your data entry screen tells you *everything* you need to know about the underlying relational design. A case of reverse engineering, perhaps. This is why I'm tending toward my idea being p–creative, because what I have come up with is such an *obvious* universal truth of relational databases. Ah, once you've thought of it, that is.

So how does the TONTO Technique work©? What's the trick behind it? After all, to claim to ignore relational theory it must just be a trick, mustn't it?

Well, there is a 'trick' to it, but it is merely one of understanding the most visible *emergent properties* of relational theory. To put it another way, relational databases, because they are based on the posit of one of one thing relating to (none, one or) many of something else, rely on drop–downs and sub–forms to work. I merely took this one stage further and decided that drop–downs and sub–forms must, logically, tell us *everything* we need to know about the underlying relational design.

This was potentially a syllogistic horror, but when it came down to it I was proved right. And to think that I used this knowledge to show off – my party piece was to look at people's data entry screens and then tell them the data model underneath; tables, relationships, the lot. I never got it wrong, either. No wonder I was never invited to parties. And then I forgot all about it except when needing to design another database. What a shame I didn't tell anyone earlier when so many have been waiting for so long for this technique. Heigh ho.

To paraphrase T. S. Eliot, sixteen years in the Shadow, stuck in limbo between the idea and the reality and between the motion and the act, is more than enough. I decided that it was time to share my idea with the world. But I suppose that I'd better, after all the hints, tell you what my idea was, all that time ago. I'll even give you a demonstration of my party piece. You'll agree that it certainly is simple. It really *can't* be an h–creative idea, can it? On the other hand, I've never come across it anywhere else.

THE IDEA

Every data entry screen tells you that there must be a table to put the data into. A drop–down on that screen tells you that there must be another table as well, from which to get the drop–down data. A sub–form on the screen tells you that there must be yet another table in which to put the sub–form data. If a sub–form has one or more drop–down, then there must be a table for each drop–down. And the simple, indisputable beauty of it is that each drop–down or sub–form tells you the exact relationship between the different tables. See the bullet points below if you haven't worked it out already, now that I've given you the idea.

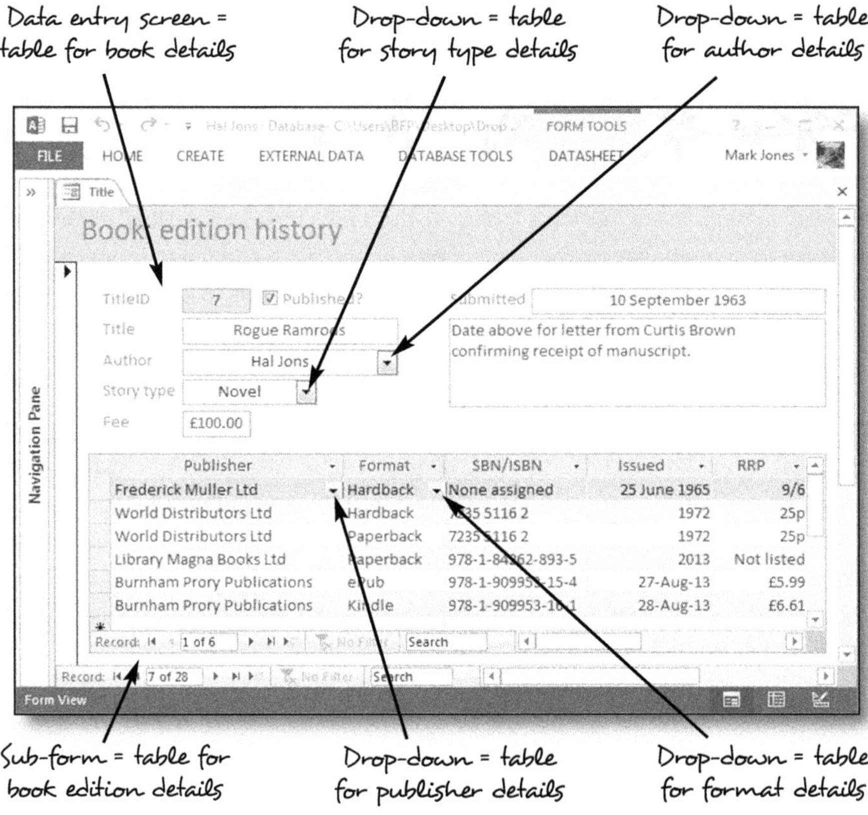

- A table created because of a drop-down will always be at the 1 end of the relationship – so, for example, the Author table will be at the 1 end and the Book table will be at the M end.
- A table created because of a sub-form will always be at the M end of the relationship – so the Book Edition table will be at the M end and the Book table will be at the 1 end. Simple!

Figure 1. My party piece.

So that was the idea. One paragraph, and a fairly short one as paragraphs go, plus a couple of bullet points. The logical extension to the idea, which came about a year later, was that, instead of using my trick to work out the relational design of existing databases I could come up with a valid relational design just by drawing the data entry screen. That worked as well. Which brought us, by very slow degrees indeed, to this book.

This idea has been staring relational database designers in the face for as long as relational design has been around (which is effectively since the publication of E. F. Codd's paper, *A Relational Model of Data for Large Shared Data Banks*, in 1970) – or, at least, since the widespread introduction of graphical user interfaces for relational databases. That anyone could have come up with the idea isn't in doubt.

I know what you're thinking – that there must be situations where the above won't hold water.

Well, two things come to mind. Firstly, that some tables identified by my technique won't become tables in the finished database; for example, a drop–down containing few items, such as *Mr*, *Mrs*, etc. True, but speaking from point of view of relational design, it is *still* a table. It is only when you move beyond relational design to the *implementation* of that design – i.e. building the database – that you make decisions to handle logical tables in different ways, such as with a combo box holding bespoke values rather than as a table look–up. However, I'll just point out that making every drop–down a table look–up makes it much easier for non–experts to add new data to the drop–down. You can't argue with that one.

Secondly, a combo box drop–down might hold a few values that are often used, whereas the majority of values entered will not be repeated so again the drop–down would only hold a few bespoke values and not look up a table. I agree that in some instances a drop–down might not denote a table – but this is not an example that would ever occur to non–experts. Remember that this book is not for experts.

Talking of which, do I deem myself a database expert on the basis of this idea and this book? Heavens forbid, I just know a fair bit about databases, that's all. I'm very aware that the world moves on and that experts tend only to remain experts in something that is pinned in time. Some clever clogs will always come up with something that makes your expertise outmoded. It'll happen to me one of these days, you just watch.

THE TONTO TECHNIQUE©

Before we move on to the essential parts of the book, it is worth looking at the traditional approach to relational database design briefly.

The traditional approach and the traditional mind-set

The traditional approach concentrates on up–front analysis and logical relational design with very little (often no) thought of how easy the subsequent database will be to use.

Generalised steps in the traditional approach:

- Undertake comprehensive analysis of the problem or opportunity situation.
- Work out what data you need in your database by looking at current data and factoring in any new required outputs.
- Make sure that the database design is fully normalised, define the keys and ensure that full referential integrity is applied.
- Identify and resolve any one–to–one and many–to–many relationships;
- Denormalise the relational design to take into account real world constraints.

Don't worry if you don't understand much, if any, of the above because you don't need to know any of it. At least, you will do all of the above using the TONTO Technique©, but without noticing.

Notice that at no time has the way in which anyone will *use* the database been taken into account in the traditional approach. End–users are generally asked what they do during bullet point 1, but they are generally not asked how they would like to do what they need to do. The problem is that user–centric design sounds good on paper, but costs more and takes more time – and both required time and costs are usually drastically under–estimated, so the concept is generally paid lip service at best or, more usually, just ignored. Which is the reason why projected cost savings, used as the driver for building the database, tend not to materialise.

Added to this, the design of the user interface – the data entry screens – is often considered infra dig or irrelevant by relational database designers and developers. It is often seen as of little importance with the task tagged on at the end of the 'real job' of doing the business analysis, relational design and back–end development.

The problem is that a badly or hastily–built interface will make even the most elegant relational design difficult to use, in which case end–users will reject the database. This might be viewed as spoiling the ship for a ha'porth of tar, but it's amazing how organisations consistently fail to learn from experience. It is no accident that the traditional mind–set often leads to data entry screens that look like Figure 2.

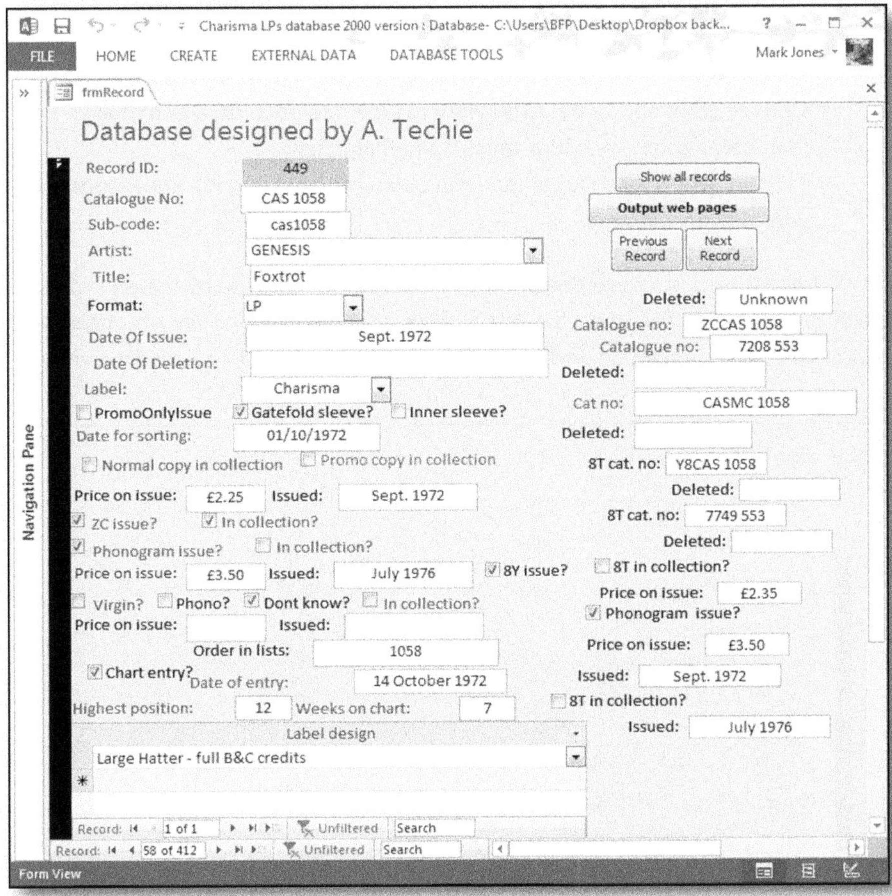

Figure 2. An example of the sort of data entry screen that end–users are often left to work with. This looks horrible and complicated to use – and the most worrying thing is that it looks as though there is lots of duplicated data, such as multiple fields for catalogue number and format information, which would be much better entered as a list. By following the TONTO Technique© the designer would have been much more likely to come up with something much nicer and easier to use.

The TONTO Technique© for turning design on its head

This method lets you decide how you want to use the database with no thought of, nor need to know about, traditional relational design tasks. Instead, you concentrate on how you want your data entry screen to look and work – and your data entry screen tells you everything you need to know about the underlying design.

The simple steps in the TONTO Technique©:

- Write down what you want your database to do, then use pen (or crayons) and paper and draw how you want your data entry screen to look.
- Decide where you want to choose your data from a drop–down or where you want to type in a list of things in a sub–form.
- Follow two simple steps to come up with your relational database design.
- Choose what sort of data you want to type into each data entry field – i.e. text, date, number, or how much something cost.
- Tidy up over a nice cup of tea (bun optional), happy in the knowledge that your design will work.

To be honest, you will have designed your relational database by the end of bullet point 3, but you've got to do the other tasks at some point before you build your database. So you might as well be introduced to them here in a pain–free way.

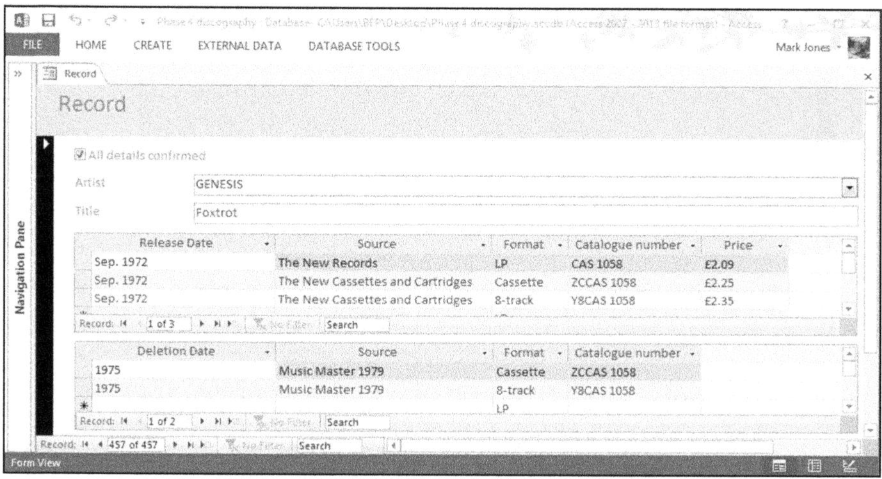

Figure 3. An example of the sort of neat and tidy data entry screen that you are likely to come up with using the TONTO Technique©. This may be because the above data entry screen *was* designed using the TONTO Technique© to solve the multiple format and catalogue number issues identified in Figure 2.

BASICS

What is a relational database and why do I want one?

These are two very good questions because, if you've got as far as picking up this book, you've probably realised that a relational database is what you either want or need. But that doesn't mean that you know the answers to the above questions, so let's answer them in stages.

What is a database?

A database is something that lets you type in, store, find and update data. It does not have to be a computer–based program or file; it could be something like a filing cabinet or card file system. The finding and updating parts are important, however, which means that the data has to be stored in a structured way so as to allow this.

What is a *relational* database?

A relational database follows the above rules and is made up of *two or more* tables, which are related together in such a way as to allow easy typing in, storage, finding and updating of data.

Why does a relational database have two or more tables?

The very simplistic answer is to make sure that your data is as accurate as possible, with no unnecessary repetition of that data. You can't do this with only one table. If you don't believe me, just look at Figures 4 and 24.

So why do I want a relational database?

Think about a non–relational database approach to storing data: for example, if you type all of your data into a spread sheet you will soon spot that you are typing the same things over and over again from row to row.

This causes two problems (see Figure 4):

> **1.** It wastes time and effort typing the same thing over and again.
> **2.** More seriously, the more often you type the same thing, the more chance you have of mistyping it; if you then search for a certain thing, the chances are that your search results will be inaccurate. In other words you will lose data.

	A	B	C	D	E	F	G
1	Artist	Title	Format	Catalogue number	Label	Country	Condition
2	KEVYN AYERS	Joy of a Toy	LP	SHVL 763	Harvest	UK	As new
3	KEVIN AYERS AND THE WHOLE WORLD	Shooting at the Moon	LP	SHSP 4005	Harvest	UK	Excellent
4	KEVIN AYERS/WHOLE WORLD	Joy of a Toy/Shooting at the Moon	2-LP	SHDW 407	Harvest	UK	Excellent
5	KEVIN AYERS & WHOLE WORLD	Hyde Park Free Concert 1970	CD	RR 002	Reel Recordings	UK	As new
6	The Beatles	With the Beatles	LP	PCS 3045	Parlophone	UK	Good
7	BEATLES, THE	Love Songs	2-LP	PCSP 721	Parlophone	UK	As new
8	BEETLES	Free as a Bird	CD single	CDR 6422	Apple	UK	As new
9	GEORGE HARRISON (Beatles on side 1)	The Best of George Harrison	LP	PAS 10011	Parlophone	UK	Very good
10	THE BEATLES	The Beatles	2-LP	PCS 7067/8	Apple	UK	VG
11	CARAVAN	In the Land of Grey and Pink	LP	PS 593	London	US	Ex
12	CARAVAN	Waterloo Lily	LP	SDL 8	Deram	UK	Excellent
13	CARVAN	Cunning Stunts	LP	SKL-R 5210	Decca	UK	As new
14	CARAVAN	Songs for Oblivion Fishermen	LP	HUX 002	Hux	UK	As new

Figure 4. Spread sheet example. Data in the *Artist*, *Format*, *Label*, *Country* and *Condition* columns is duplicated from record to record. Also, some data in the *Artist* and *Condition* columns that is supposed to be the same is entered inconsistently.

What a relational database does is to break up your data into groups of different *things*, so that one table holds data about one thing, the next table data about a different thing and so on. The number of tables is dependent on the number of things that you need to hold data about. There's more to it than this, but you really don't need to know about it.

The upshot of breaking things up is that you only type data in once and, the next time you need to enter the same data, you choose it from a drop–down. This ensures two things, both of them good:

> **1.** Your data will be entered consistently over time, meaning that search results will be accurate. In other words, you will not lose any of your data.
> **2.** It prevents you from accidentally adding random things – if you haven't already got something in a drop–down, then you can't enter it by mistake when you use that drop–down.

But what if I *want* to add something that's not in the drop-down?

Simple. First you add it to the drop–down. Then you choose it from the drop–down.

If I've broken up all my data, how do I join it together again?

This is where the *relational* bit of relational databases comes in. The separate tables are joined together in the background by relationships. When you build the database, your data entry screen shows the data joined back up again – in fact, you'd never know that it was all split up if you weren't reading this. If you need to, you can also print out the data in joined–up fashion by building what are called queries. But this only works if you get the relational design right.

Okay, I've sort of understood all this but, at the end of the day, does it *really* matter if I get the design wrong?

Let's just say that if the design is flawed, then the database will be either stupidly hard to use and provide you with inaccurate data or, if you're *lucky*, will just not work. Is that a plain enough answer?

Getting the design right before you start to build the database is the most important part. It is vital. So that's a *yes*. The trouble is that getting the design right has always been the hard bit. But this book gives you the best chance to be sure that your design is right.

BAD DATA IS BAD NEWS FOR RESEARCH

If you use a relational database to store and process your research data and you get the relational design even slightly wrong, then you can't trust your research results. It's that simple.

Perhaps research funding bodies and institutions at which research takes place should be worried. Not taking relational database design seriously (i.e. by leaving researchers to design their own databases) can severely affect the credibility of resultant research findings and of any subsequent research based on those findings.

There are some things you can't get away without

Even with this simple technique, these are still relational databases we're designing, which means that there are some things you have to either do or otherwise know about. There's no getting away with these things; they go with the territory.

The good thing is that, when it comes to relational designs and keys, you need to know about them but you don't have to understand the logic behind how they work – indeed, I won't bore you with this in any case. As for data entry fields, the only thing you need to know is very simple to comprehend, so we'll start with that.

Data entry fields – small is beautiful

To save lots of problems later on, you must:

- Split your data up into small (though sensible) pieces.

It is extremely simple to join two or more data entry fields together if you need to, but it is very difficult to split a single field up later on.

TYPICAL PROBLEMS WITH SORTING DATA

If you have a single field for the artist's name, you might want to type in such items as The Beatles, Kevin Ayers, Traffic *and so on. The problem with just one field is that if you want to sort your data alphabetically you will end up with both* The Beatles *and* Traffic *appearing under "T". Similarly,* Kevin Ayers *would appear under "K" instead of "A". By splitting up data into smaller parts, you can have one field for either surname or band name, e.g.* Beatles *and* Ayers, *and another field for* The *and* Kevin. *All your sorts will then work perfectly.*

The most common problems are generally to do with names (as per tip above) and addresses. Always split up addresses into multiple fields and always have specifically–named fields for items like town and postcode so you know which fields to search.

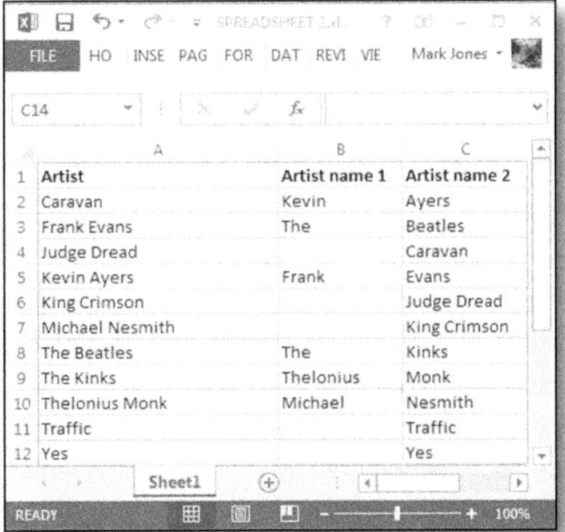

	A	B	C
1	**Artist**	**Artist name 1**	**Artist name 2**
2	Caravan	Kevin	Ayers
3	Frank Evans	The	Beatles
4	Judge Dread		Caravan
5	Kevin Ayers	Frank	Evans
6	King Crimson		Judge Dread
7	Michael Nesmith		King Crimson
8	The Beatles	The	Kinks
9	The Kinks	Thelonius	Monk
10	Thelonius Monk	Michael	Nesmith
11	Traffic		Traffic
12	Yes		Yes

Figure 5. One field for artist (left) will result in an incorrect sort. Two fields for artist (right) will result in a correct sort. I'll leave it to you to argue as to whether *Judge Dread* should appear under *J* or *D*!

Relational designs and how to draw them

Relational databases work on the principle that one of something relates to many of something else, such as *one* singer can release *many* records or *one* parasite can cause *many* symptoms.

When it comes to relational designs all you need to be able to do is:

1. Draw two rectangular boxes and give them names.
2. Add a relatively straight line between them (i.e. the relationship).
3. Write "1" at one end of the relationship and "M" at the other.
4. Repeat the above as many times as necessary (you'll know when you're done).

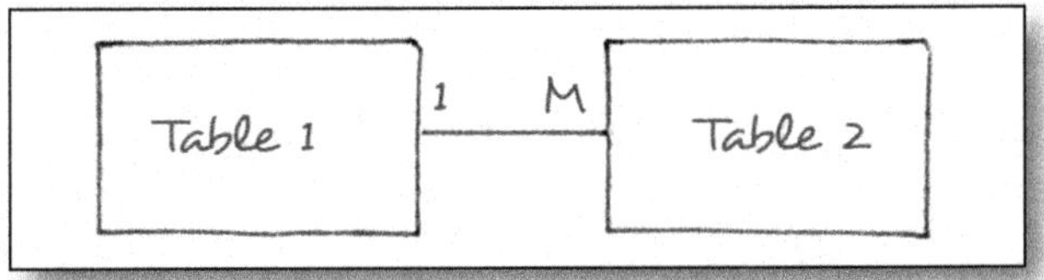

Figure 6. Drawing tables and relationships is this simple. Hand–drawn is best until you've come up with the whole design, at which point you can happily recreate the design digitally (and more neatly).

The TONTO Technique© tells you which boxes to draw, which specific ones to draw lines between as well as which end of the line is the 1 end and which is the M end.

Keys, and where to put them

Keys are what make relational databases work, so you have to get them right. Luckily, the rules relating to keys are few and simple:

> **1.** Every table in your database must have a key, which lets you uniquely identify every record in each table (see note below). This is called the *primary key*.
> **2.** The primary key from the 1 end of a relationship has to be placed at the M end of any relationship as well. The key you place at the M end is called a *foreign key*.
> **3.** The key at each end of the relationship must be set for the same type of data, so if the primary key is set for text, then the foreign key must also be set for text.

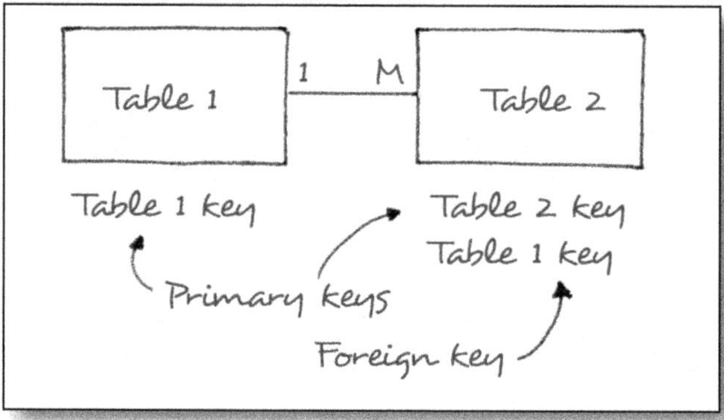

Figure 7. Every table has a primary key and you always add the primary key from the 1 end of any relationship to any tables at the M end.

Don't worry about understanding any of the above. Knowing what to do is far more important than understanding why you need to do it.

> **WHAT MAKES A GOOD PRIMARY KEY?**
>
> *Basically, the key in each table must be something that will never be repeated. A good example of things that are unique in the UK are National Insurance numbers. Everyone is assigned a National Insurance number when they are born. No two National Insurance Numbers should be the same. Therefore, this would be an excellent choice of key in a Person table. (We'll see see some examples of bad primary keys later on.)*

WORKED EXAMPLE

The main worked example explains the TONTO Technique© as it goes, whilst the two further worked examples only include explanations where there is something that has not been covered previously or to point out issues that are encountered often. A single database example could never cover all likely scenarios, at least, not without being heavily contrived, but with the three different real–world examples on offer the most common issues and 'gotchas' are covered off. The suggestion is that you work – or at least read – through all three examples.

Just a couple of pointers. Firstly, don't necessarily expect to get the scenario right first go. There will always be something that you forget to add – that or you will add things that are not necessarily relevant, such as requirements for how the database will work rather than the things you need to do with the data. My advice is not to worry too much about it. Even real database designers work out what they've forgotten when they start to build the database. The research database example is a case in point and some extra data fields had to be added toward the end of the design phase.

Secondly, it is possible that remembering something once you've gone through the whole set of steps means starting again. Don't despair, this too is something that almost always happens at least once. The joy is that starting again is a matter of taking a couple of hours longer (which just means more tea and another bun using this technique). Using traditional methods this can take out whole days; weeks even. Even for relational designers that know what they're doing.

Meanwhile, another suggestion is that you work through this section using your own example. Go on, be daring.

Step 0. Are you already capturing data in some way?

If the answer is yes, have a look at your current data recording method:

Records by Artist

Artist name: The Beatles Genre: 1960s popular

Records

Title	Format	Cat. no.	Label	Country	Condition	Date bought	Cost
With The Beatles	LP	PCS 3045	Parlophone	UK	VG	23/2/78	£2.50
The Beatles	2-LP	PCS 7067/8	Apple	UK	EX	1/3/79	£3.00
Abbey Road	Reel to Reel	L 383	Apple	US	As New	24/5/79	£1.75
Help	Cassette	TCPCS 3071	Parlophone	UK	EX	24/5/79	£1.00
Magical Mystery Tour	LP	MAL 2835	Capitol	US	VG	8/5/80	£3.00
Love Songs	2-LP	PCSP 721	Parlophone	UK	VG	15/5/80	£3.00
Rock 'n' Roll Music	2-LP	PCSP 719	Parlophone	UK	EX	23/5/80	£1.00
Hey Jude	LP	CPCS 106	Apple	UK (export)	As New	1/7/81	£5.00

Figure 8. Example of a paper–based form listing records by an individual artist. In this approach there would be one sheet (or more sheets, depending on the number of records by particular artists in the collection) for every artist.

If you have a paper form, computer–based spread sheet, a long list on paper or a card filing system then you have probably spotted that you often type or write the same things over and over again – make a note of all the places where you type or write the same things over and over again and return to this note for step 2. Basically, repeating data is what relational databases are designed to solve.

If you have a paper form that you are using to record data, such as in Figure 8 above, then this might already be designed in a similar way to how you will want your data entry screen set out. Basically, well–designed data entry screens tend to mimic well–designed paper forms. That's why data entry screens are called *forms*. That's also why it is best to design data entry screens on paper first.

If you are coming to this task data–free, then don't worry. Coming with a fresh pair of eyes and a mind untrammelled by previous attempts to record your data is not a problem. It just means that, come steps 3 and 4, that you will probably take a bit longer. We are only talking minutes, so it's no big deal.

Step 1. The scenario

Write down what you want the database to do – a few bullet points or a paragraph or two will generally do. The reason is just to have something to look back at to make sure that you haven't forgotten anything during later steps. The first example scenario for this book is as follows:

> *I need to keep a record of my music collection for insurance purposes. I want to keep a record of every artist in my collection, along with a list of every record I have by them, whatever the format – LP, CD, cassette, 7" single, one–off track digital download, flexi disc, etc. So that I can assign the correct value to each individual record, I need to be able to record the catalogue number, format, record label, label design and condition, plus any additional information that might affect value. I also want to know when I bought the record and how much it cost me. It would be quite nice to assign each artist with a genre too, if that's not too difficult.*

It's always worth looking through your scenario to see if there's anything that doesn't have any impact on the relational design. Often things like calculations and printouts are mentioned but, in database terms, these are outputs. If it's nothing to do with the data that the database needs to hold, then it isn't relevant at this point; though keep it in mind for when you come to *build* the database.

That said, however, printouts and calculations can still tell you something about the data you need in your database. The database needs to hold the data that will be used on the printout; also it will need to hold the data with which you need to do any calculations. So required outputs are good for hinting at some of the bits that you may have forgotten to write down.

> **GET STARTED NOW**
>
> *Why not write down your own scenario and requirements now and follow the rest of the steps using your own example?*

Step 2. Draw your data entry screen

Small–scale databases tend to have just one main data entry screen, but if you want to type in your data using more than one screen, then there's nothing to stop you. In steps 3 and 4, you will just have to do the tasks for each screen instead of just for one, that's all.

> **MORE THAN ONE DATA ENTRY SCREEN?**
>
> *If you have drawn more than one data entry screen, you will come up with some of the same tables and relationships between two or more screens. This is perfectly normal – but just make sure that you don't give the same table two different names! See the final worked example for using the TONTO Technique© with more than one data entry screen.*

The following screenshots show some real world, small–scale database, data entry screens (fake data is used in the last example for reasons of data security). Remember that, unlike spread sheets, data entry screens show you one record at a time. For example, in the screenshot directly below the screen shows you data about just one postcard. When you go to the next record, the screen will be exactly the same but the postcard documented will be different as will all the related data about that postcard.

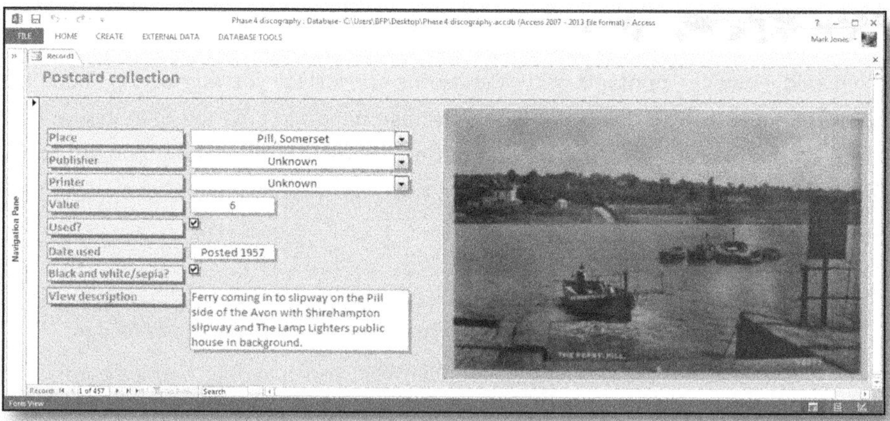

Figure 9. Postcard database with three drop–downs and no sub–form (and linked image file).

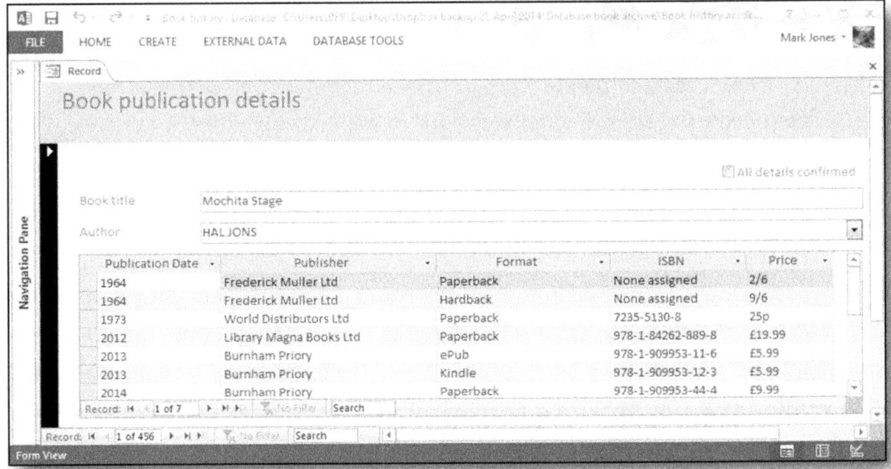

Figure 10. Book collection database with drop–down and subform. the second and third sub–form fields have drop–downs. Depending on how a database is built, sub–form drop–downs may only appear when you tab or click into that field. Drop–downs on the main form are generally always visible.

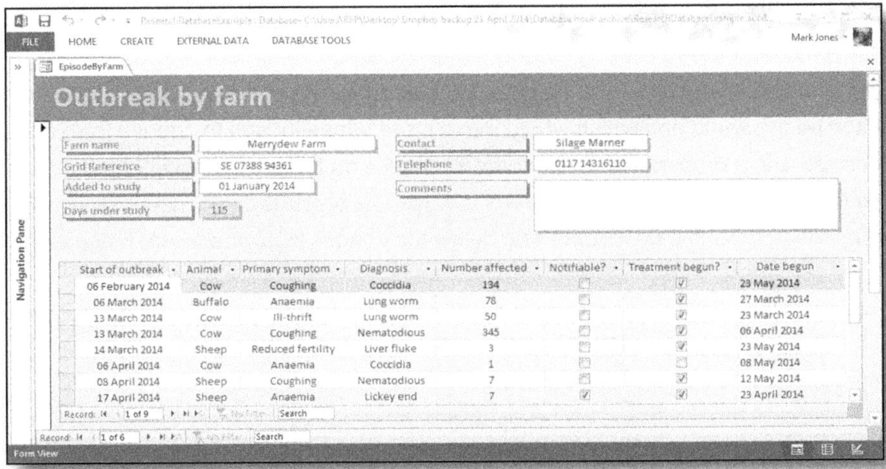

Figure 11. Research database with sub–form. Second, third and fourth sub–form fields are drop–downs.

REAL WORLD INTRUSION

Note that the examples shown are relatively neat and well laid out. If you have ever used a corporate (i.e. big business) database, you will know that data entry screens are often very hard to use because either things are named in ways that make no sense to you or you have to constantly move between multiple screens to get your data in – or indeed any of myriad other horrors that make life hard for the database user.

In light of the above real world intrusion, when you put pencil, pen, crayon or felt–tip to paper in a minute or so, don't think in terms of any horrible data entry screens you might ever have seen or been forced to use. Remember that you are designing your database for you, so draw a screen that will make it easy to type in your data.

Don't forget to break your data up into the smallest useful parts. Also, show where you want a drop–down or where you want to add to a list in a sub–form. If you find that you don't need at least one drop–down and/or at least one sub–form, then you probably only need a spread sheet.

If you are already recording data, go back to the note you made at step 0 about places where you constantly type or write the same thing over and over again. If you don't have any pre–existing data, think about which of those pieces of data will often be the same and which would make more sense for you to choose from a set of options in a drop–down. Look at the examples on the previous two pages to see some examples of where drop–downs are used (sub–forms do not necessarily show drop–downs, but the descriptive text below the images indicates where these exist).

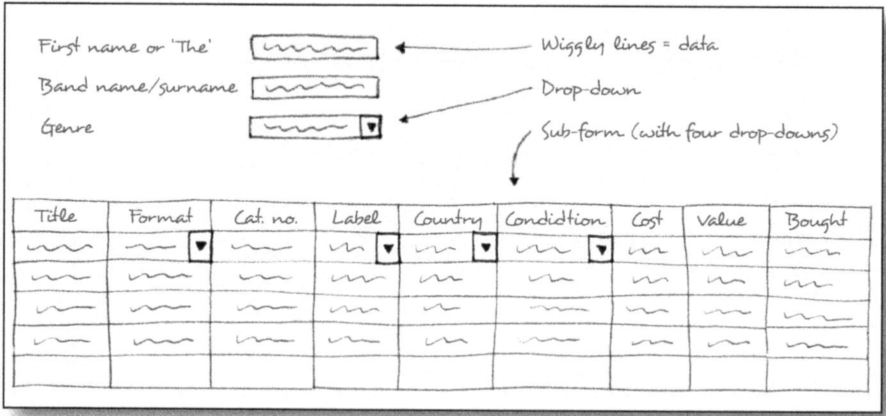

Figure 12. Designing your data entry screen on paper doesn't necessarily require advanced artistic skills; for the later examples I used a ruler, but for this one I didn't bother! This really is 'back–of–bus–ticket stuff!

Step 3. The clever bit

IGNORE SUB–FORMS FOR THE MOMENT

If you have any sub–forms on your hand–drawn design, then just ignore them for the moment; we'll come to sub–forms in the following step.

If you read the *Background* section, this will be old news to you. If you skipped that section, just remember that **wherever there is a data entry screen, there has to be a table to put that data into**. In this instance, you are recording data about recording artists, so you already know one database table – *Artist*.

You also know the data entry fields in the *Artist* table because there they are on your data entry screen – these are the two fields for the artist's name and the *Genre* field. Call these *Artist name 1*, *Artist name 2* and *Genre* for the moment – we will need to revisit names later on, but these will do for now. So what we have is:

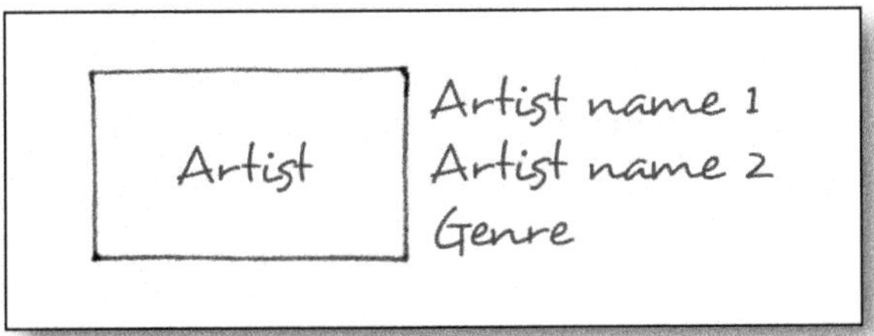

Figure 13. The first identified table in your relational database design along with the data entry fields. Don't worry about adding keys yet because this needs to be looked at later when you have the whole design.

Now we need to work out what other tables there are and what the relationships are between these tables. Nothing could be simpler.

Look at where you want to select data from a drop–down

It's time to look at any drop–downs in your data entry screen design. Remember that **every drop–down means that you need another table**.

In this instance, this looks to be just *Genre*. So, now you have two tables – *Artist* and *Genre*.

EVERY DATA ENTRY SCREEN IS DIFFERENT

Every database is different and other databases could have more than one dropdown on the main part of the screen. Look back at Figure 9 – that one has three drop–downs; which means three other tables – yes, it's that simple and works this way every time.

Even though we've already got the *Genre* field in the *Artist* table, we put it into the *Genre* table as well – you do this every time; **wherever you have a drop–down, the drop–down field goes in both tables**. If you think that this is starting to sound like the *primary* and *foreign* examples of a key, then you could be right.

There may possibly need to be other data entry fields in the *Genre* table, but we'll leave that until the last step.

Was that the clever bit?

Well, it's fairly clever, but the really clever bit is that the drop–down tells you what the relationship is between *Artist* and *Genre* – **the new table created because of a drop-down is always at the 1 end of the relationship**.

So the table created because of the drop–down, *Genre*, is at the 1 end of the relationship, and *Artist* is at the M end. In real terms, what this means is that each item in the *Genre* table is typed in once only (as in 'one'), but can then be chosen for more than one artist in the *Artist* table (as in 'many').

That's the really clever bit – and it works exactly the same way every time. So what you have at this point is:

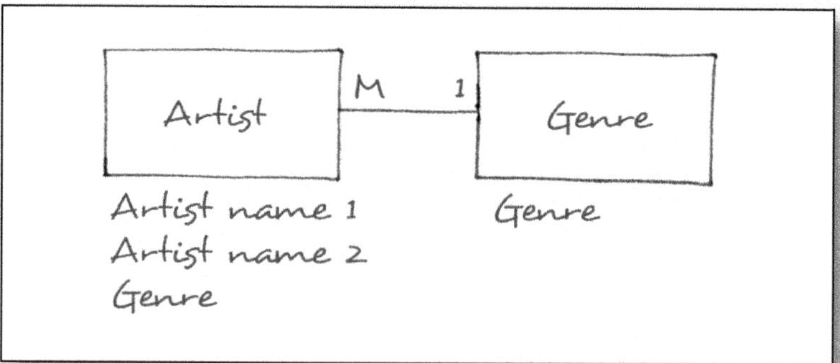

Figure 14. The clever bit shows you explicitly what the relationship is between two tables.

Step 4. The other clever bit

Now it's time to look at any sub–forms in your data entry screen design. **Every sub–form means that you need another table**.

So what are we recording data about in the sub–form in the example screen design? This is where you will type in the details of the records released by the artist shown in the main part of your form. So now we have a third table, which is *Record.*

The second really clever bit is that the sub–form tells you what the relationship is between *Artist* and *Record* because **the new table created because of a sub–form is always at the M end of the relationship**.

So the *Record* table is at the M end of the relationship and *Artist* is at the 1 end. Again, this works exactly the same way every time.

As to what fields go into the *Record* table, that is every field you can see in the sub–form, which gives you:

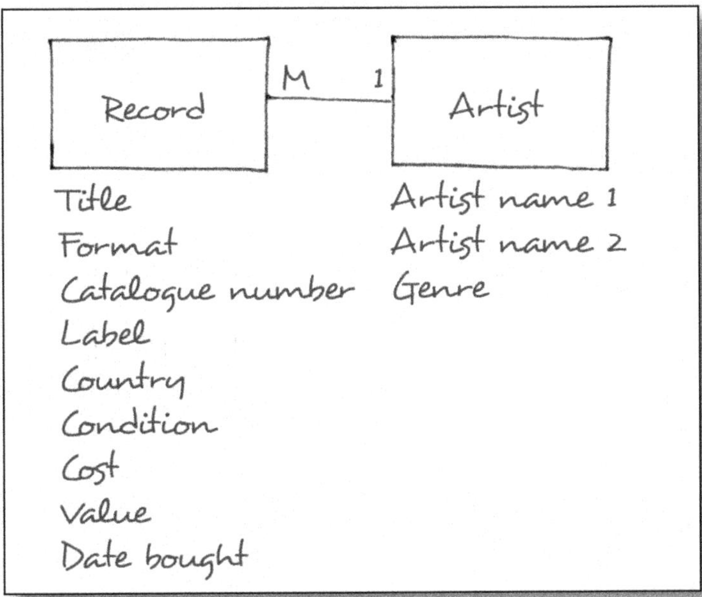

Figure 15. The relationship between the newly–identified Record table and the Artist table, complete with the data entry fields that fit in the respective tables.

Now let's look at the sub–form again. Are there data items that you would want to choose from a drop–down? Yes, *Label*, *Format*, *Country* and *Condition* will all have the same things typed into them over and over. So, following the rule from step 3, this tells you that *Label*, *Format*, *Country* and *Condition* are all tables. The only difference is that these tables are not related to the *Artist* table – it is the sub–form table that they are related to, which is *Record.*

RULE OF THUMB # 1

But won't you be typing the same pieces of data into Title, Date bought, Value and Cost? Should they be tables too? A very useful Rule of Thumb says that anything that has a handful of repeating data items but which is potentially infinitely variable, such as dates or money (in fact lots of things to do with numbers generally), will not be a table.

Use the rule from step 3 to work out the relationships between *Record* and the four new tables. That's right, *Record* must be at the M end, because the rest are tables created because of drop–downs. So *Label*, *Format*, *Country* and *Condition* are all at the 1 end of their respective relationships. Use the rule to work out which fields appear at both ends. Yes, the *Label* table will include the *Label* data entry field (as does the *Record* table of course)...and so on for the other three tables.

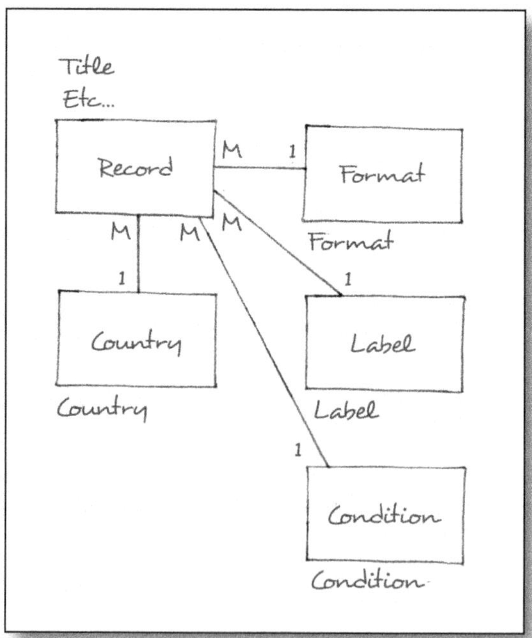

Figure 16. Tables identified from drop–downs in the sub–form along with relationships and data entry fields.

So, join all the bits together (without the data entry fields, just too keep things neat) and what you have is:

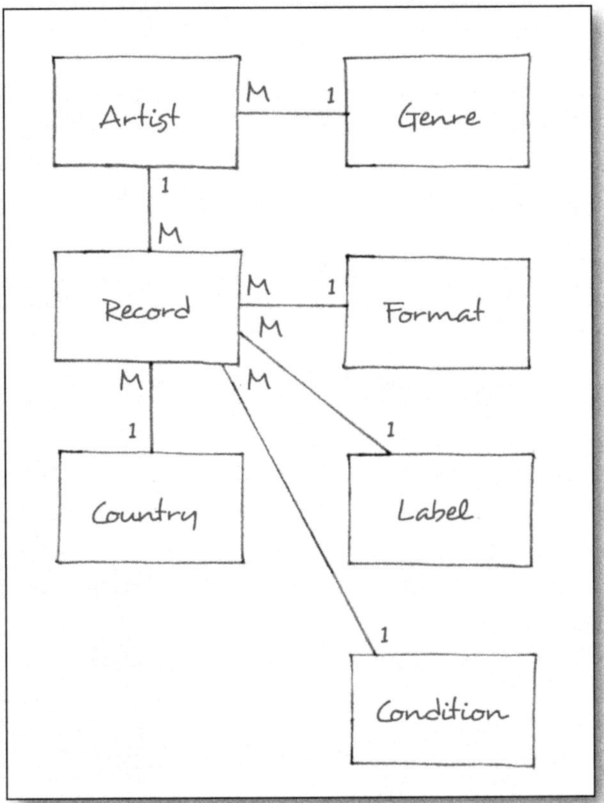

Figure 17. A perfect relational design showing all identified tables along with the relationships between those tables.

Guess what, *you have just designed your first relational database*. Did it hurt? Doing it the traditional way is a lot less fun, believe me.

There are still a couple of things to do before you are ready to start building the database. So even though this is nothing to do with the TONTO Technique©, we might as well do these tasks here in easy–to–follow fashion.

Step 5. Tidy up the keys

The section earlier pointing out the rules for keys made it fairly clear that every table has to have a primary key and that the key from the 1 end of the relationship also has to appear at the M end, where it is known as a foreign key.

We already know which tables are related to which, based on using the clever bits of the TONTO Technique©, and we even have a pretty good idea of most of the keys based on the places where we put the same data entry field in two tables. Now we just have to tidy up the keys because we have a few gaps.

THINKING CAP ON STANDBY ALERT

What I haven't told you yet is that you need to do a spot of thinking at this point. Not much, but a bit.

The key, remember, has to individually identify every record in the table, so you need to look at each table to see if any of the pre–existing data entry fields will do the job of uniquely identifying every individual record in that table. If not you can add an auto number field to the table. An auto number just adds 1 every time you add a new record, so the first record in your table will have a primary key value of 1, the second will be 2 and so on. You don't have to type these in, the database does it for you.

OTHER OPTIONS FOR PRIMARY KEYS

There are two alternatives to using an auto number field, though these tend to be for specialist cases. On the one hand you could create your own never–repeated code and create a key field using that instead; if so, you will have to work out some way of defining your code. You could also make the key from more than one field – i.e. if there are two or more fields that, taken together, will never be repeated. Both of these options can offer what is called validation *(i.e. preventing you from accidentally typing in the same record twice) but are only for those that really know what they're doing.*

Let's look at each table in turn to see if there is anything that already individually identifies each record in that table. If not, then we'll add an auto number field. Before we start, though, there are some easy–to–make mistakes when it comes to choosing primary key fields – see the following 'gotcha' examples.

NOTED 'GOTCHAS' WHEN CHOOSING KEYS

Be wary of names of things (and people), product codes and similar. In this current database Title *or* Catalogue number *might look to be good contenders for primary key in the* Record *table. However, choosing either would stop you from entering details of two or more copies of the same record – and I've never seen a serious collection yet without several copies of something or other.*

Also, titles and catalogue numbers can both be reused. For example, Peter Gabriel's first four LPs were all simply titled Peter Gabriel *and his record label, Charisma, had a happily–haphazard habit of accidentally reusing catalogue numbers on different records.*

Artist

There is no field that can uniquely identify every artist in the table, so add an auto number field and call it *Artist key* or some such.

Following the rule for keys, add *Artist key* (which is at the 1 end of the relationship) to the *Record* table (at the M end).

Genre

No two genres (e.g. *Reggae*, *Jazz*, *Folk*, etc.) will be the same so you can make *Genre* the key field. I think we'd already guessed this, because we also have *Genre* in the *Artist* table. So, in *Artist*, *Genre* is a foreign key.

Record

There is no field that can uniquely identify every record in the table (if you disagree, see Noted 'gotchas' above) so add an auto number field and call it *Record key*.

There is no relationship where *Record* appears at the 1 end, so *Record key* does not need to be put in any other table.

Format

No two formats (e.g. *LP*, *7" single*, *CD*, etc.) will be the same so you can make *Format* the key field. Notice that we already have *Format* in the Record table as well, where it represents a foreign key.

Country

No two countries (e.g. *UK*, *US*, *Germany*, etc.) will be the same so you can make *Country* the key field. Notice that we already have *Country* in the Record table as well, where it represents a foreign key.

Label

No two labels (e.g. *Harvest*, *Virgin*, *Parlophone*, etc.) will be the same so you can make *Label* the key field. Notice that we already have *Label* in the Record table as well, where it represents a foreign key.

Condition

No two conditions (e.g. *As new*, *Excellent*, *Very good*, etc.) will be the same so you can make *Condition* the key field. Notice that we already have *Condition* in the Record table as well, where it represents a foreign key.

IMPORTANT EXCEPTION: NAMES IN DROP–DOWNS

The above is all very well, but there are some 'problems' if in your own design you want to choose someone's name from a drop–down. Lots of people have the same name as other people so in a table holding data about people a name in itself cannot be guaranteed to uniquely identify every individual. Also, you can only choose one data item from a drop–down, whereas, as we've already seen, names should always be broken down into two separate fields (three if middle names are important to you).

There is a simple solution, which is to add an auto number field as the primary key in a table holding data about people and then add a number (long integer) field as the foreign key to the table at the other end of the relationship (i.e the M *end). Relational database software let's you still see the names instead of the numbers.*

The final two example scenarios include choosing names from drop–downs, so have a look at these to see how the issue is dealt with.

Step 6. Choose data types and decide on size/format

There are three parts to this, all of which are fairly simple:

1. Decide what type of data each data entry field will hold.
2. Decide how you want the data to look or work (i.e. format).
3. Decide how big each data entry field has to be.

When it comes to keys, there is one very important thing that you have to do, which is to give your primary and foreign keys the same data type. It also helps enormously to make them the same size and format as well. When it comes to auto number primary keys, see the tip below.

AUTO NUMBERS AND DATA TYPE

If the key at the 1 *end of the relationship is an* auto number, *then the foreign key at the* M *end of the relationship must be a* Number, *set as* Long Integer. *This is because auto numbers are long integers.*

Most data entry fields will be textual or numeric, though there are other types. The list below shows the data types available in the current version of Microsoft Access.

LIST OF MICROSOFT ACCESS DATA TYPES

SHORT TEXT: *text up to 255 characters (this data type is called 'Text' in Access 2010 and earlier versions)*
LONG TEXT: *for larger amounts of text (this data type is called 'Memo' in Access 2010 and earlier versions)*
NUMBER: *generally use only when you want to do a calculation:* Long Integer *is the most commonly–used format for whole numbers;* Double *is the most commonly–used format for numbers requiring decimal places; other formats are available for more specialised needs*
DATE/TIME: *self–explanatory (use Short Text if you want to enter year only)*
CURRENCY: *self–explanatory*
AUTONUMBER: *only useful for primary keys*
YES/NO: *tick box where you only have two options to choose from*
OLE OBJECT: *this is to hold other files, such as images, in tables but best to use the Attachment option instead*
HYPERLINK: *can be either to a local file or to a web location*
ATTACHMENT: *links to files without bloating your database by storing the linked files inside your database.*
CALCULATED: *new option to create calculations in a table; avoid unless you really know what you're doing*

Most of the above data types are fairly straightforward to decide upon, but number fields can be a bit trickier – use the following rule of thumb.

RULE OF THUMB # 2

Even if the data in a particular field will be a number, it is best to leave it as a text field unless you are going to do some sort of calculation with that particular field.

The above rule of thumb is very useful so as to preclude lots of potential issues with things like telephone and fax numbers. These items are undoubtedly numeric, but often start with a zero. If you set the data type as number, then the database will cheerfully strip off any preceding zeros, which tend to be important to telephone numbers. A text field, on the other hand, won't remove anything.

As for deciding how you want the data to look, this is mostly cosmetic. For example, you can choose for a date to be displayed in various formats according to taste, such as *10/11/2014* or *10 November 2014*. But there can be issues with dates – see the following tip.

DATE FORMAT ISSUE

Choosing to see the month as a word precludes the confusion often caused by the difference in display between different country's date formats – for example, does 10/11/2014 mean 10 November or 11 October?

When it comes to number fields, different options let you do certain things. For example, if you choose an integer–style format for a number field, then you can only type in whole numbers (go and do a Google search on *integer* if you don't know why). Other formats will determine whether you can have decimal places and also determine how many decimal places you can have.

With text fields, you need to decide how big to make the field – in other words, how many characters you can type in. This is because databases are fairly stupid in some ways. They don't necessarily look at the amount of data you have typed into each text field, but assume that every text field is filled to the size that you assigned to it and so the database can get VERY BIG even without much in the way of data.

Microsoft Access 2013 assigns a default field size of 255 characters to *small text* fields. So, if you're only ever going to be typing in *Mr*, *Mrs*, *Miss*, *Ms* or *Dr* then you are using at least 251 characters too many for every record.

What happens, though, if you make the field 4 characters long and later need to enter *Professor*? Well, here's where another useful rule of thumb comes in.

RULE OF THUMB # 3

Think of the largest piece of text that you are likely to enter into any particular text field and add 10. If it is well under 10 characters, then make it 10, or even 15 characters long. It is best to over–estimate during design.

Each table might look like the following – field names come first, followed by data type and then size and/or format. *PK* after the name denotes that the field is the primary key and *FK* denotes that it is a foreign key. The convention I learned back in 1996 stated that you list any foreign keys in a table directly after the primary key, so who am I to argue?

Table	Field name (key)	Data type	Size/format
Artist	Artist key (PK)	Auto Number	Default
	Genre (FK)	Short Text	30
	Artist name 1	Short Text	100
	Artist name 2	Short Text	100
Condition	Condition (PK)	Short Text	20
Country	Country (PK)	Short Text	50
Format	Format (PK)	Short Text	30
Genre	Genre (PK)	Short Text	30
Label	Label (PK)	Short Text	100
Record	Record key (PK)	Auto Number	Default
	Artist key (FK)	Number	Long Integer
	Condition (FK)	Short Text	20
	Country (FK)	Short Text	50
	Format (FK)	Short Text	30
	Label (FK)	Short Text	100
	Title	Short Text	255
	Catalogue number	Short Text	30
	Cost	Currency	£
	Value	Currency	£
	Date bought	Date/Time	Long Date

Table 1. Record collection database tables, fields and properties prior to tidying up.

Step 7. Tidy up over a nice cup of tea (bun optional)

Anything to add?

Have a look at your tables. Is there any other information that you want to record about *Artist*, *Record*, *Genre*, *Format*, *Label* or *Condition*?

If in doubt, 'comments' fields are always good things to add. If, later, you find that you are constantly typing the same things into a comments field, then that tells you that you probably forgot a field. Never mind because you can always add extra fields to tables and data entry screens later if you got your relational design correct – and using the TONTO Technique©, you really *should* have a correct design.

If you want to add another data entry field, have a think about whether you would want to be able to choose the data from a drop–down or whether you would want to add it as a list in a sub–form. It might be that the new piece of data means another table. If so, just go back and follow the rules in steps 3 and/or 4.

Something to keep in mind is that if you want to choose the name of a person or company from a drop–down then you will almost certainly want contact details for that person or company. So any *Person*, *Company*, *Supplier* or *Customer* table you identify from a drop–down will almost always include address and other contact details. You may want an extra data entry screen to enter these details, but it's up to you. You can always add details directly into the table if you want and just stick with one data entry screen for your main data entry needs.

Calculations

Are any of the pieces of data you want on your data entry screen or in any sub–forms calculations? If so, these have nothing to do with any tables. (Note that as from Microsoft Access 2013 you can create specific calculations in tables, but this option is currently limited and is not for beginners.)

If you've added any calculations to any of your tables, remove them! When it comes to calculations, what you need to make sure is that, somewhere or other, you have the data with which to do the calculation. For example, in the current database, you could easily find out how much your entire record collection is worth because you have a field with current value. A simple query will add up all of the values you have (and ignore any where you don't know the value). Similarly, you could calculate how much profit you might make on each record because you have fields for both original cost and current value.

Naming data entry fields and tables

Every data entry field and every table has to have a name, but there are three things to either think about or to avoid:

> **1.** Give every data entry field and table a sensible name that tells you what it is – but take into account the following two rules.
> **2.** Don't use gaps or symbols.
> **3.** Don't use *reserved words*.

Sensible names

If you have a series of data entry fields such as *Address 1*, *Address 2*, *Address 3*, *Address 4*, *Address 5* and *Address 6* how do you know which one to search to find, for example, everyone from London? If you name your fields along the lines of *Address1* (no gap – see below), *Address2*, *Address3*, *Town*, *Postcode*, *Country* then you will make searches much easier because you will know what to find where.

Gaps and symbols

Gaps or symbols in names can cause real problems. As for gaps, rather than use a name like *Artist name 1*, use *ArtistName1*. This can be inelegant, but ignoring this rule can mean building a database that continuously throws up incomprehensible error messages or refuses to work. Remember that on your data entry screen, you can call the data entry field anything you like because it's only a label you see, not the actual field name.

As for symbols (e.g. *!*, *"*, *£*, *$*, *%*), don't use any. Note that although the underscore symbol (e.g. *_*) can be used in names in MS Access this may not be acceptable in other database software applications.

Reserved words

These are commands that database software uses in the background to make the database work. The trouble is that reserved words tend to be exactly the sort of words that you are likely to want to use for naming things with – words like *Name*, *Date*, *Year* and so on. To find a list of reserved words, search online for the name of your software and "reserved words" – e.g. *"Access 2013" +"reserved words"* – including the plus sign and speech–marks.

So, with a bit of a tidy up, here's what you've now got.

Table	Field name (key)	Data type	Size/format
Artist	ArtistKey (PK)	Auto Number	Default
	Genre (FK)	Short Text	30
	ArtistName1	Short Text	100
	ArtistName2	Short Text	100
	Comments	Long Text	Default
Condition	Condition (PK)	Short Text	20
	Comments	Long Text	Default
Country	Country (PK)	Short Text	50
	Comments	Long Text	Default
Format	Format (PK)	Short Text	30
	Comments	Long Text	Default
Genre	Genre (PK)	Short Text	30
	Comments	Long Text	Default
Label	Label (PK)	Short Text	100
	Comments	Long Text	Default
Record	RecordKey (PK)	Auto Number	Default
	ArtistKey (FK)	Number	Long Integer
	Condition (FK)	Short Text	20
	Country (FK)	Short Text	50
	Format (FK)	Short Text	30
	Label (FK)	Short Text	100
	Title	Short Text	255
	CatalogueNumber	Short Text	30
	Cost	Currency	£
	Value	Currency	£
	DateBought	Date/Time	Long Date
	Comments	Long Text	Default

Table 2. Record collection database tables, fields and properties with database–friendly names.

IS THAT IT?

Yes. That really is all there is to it – for small–scale relational databases at any rate. Corporate, organisation–wide databases tend to have a few more issues to solve (understatement) before you can go ahead and build the thing but in terms of said small–scale, relational databases you have now done everything you need to do.

You have designed your database from point of view of tables, relationships and keys, which is the part that most people get wrong using either traditional relational theory or the received wisdom propogated by certain software companies that you don't need to know anything about relational theory to use their database products. (Hey, what do you know? They were right all along! It just needed this technique, that's all.)

You have also designed how you want your database to look – and decided what sorts of data will go in each data entry field. You've also given the data entry fields (and tables) sensible names that will not cause any problems and which will help you to use the database more easily when built.

WHAT'S NEXT?

There are two things to do next:

1. Read or work through the following two scenarios, based around real–world small business and research examples, to see how some common issues, such as wanting names in drop–dows, are dealt with. The research example in particular shows how things can start to get a bit more confusing where you have a need for multiple sub–forms in your data entry screen.
2. Build the database that you've just designed. This shouldn't be a problem because there's another book, once more in simple, no–nonsense language that tells you how.

Relational Database Development Made Easy takes the three relational database designs developed in this book and shows how to build each one using Microsoft Access 2013.

I know what you're thinking. Your own database won't be the same as the ones in the book. Well, that doesn't matter because what *Relational Database Development Made Easy* does is to show you the *building blocks* for building *any* database from a paper–based design.

It has to use one database or another as an example, so it seemed fairly sensible to use the ones designed in this book.

Further information about the book is available on page 70.

FURTHER EXAMPLES

This section explicitly shows how to deal with names in drop–downs and highlights a few common issues that tend to crop up. As mentioned earlier, just one example could never cover everything that you are likely to encounter, but using three examples provides at least a little more scope. Also, the second of these two examples adds a certain amount of complexity by introducing a requirement for both multiple data entry screens and for multiple sub–forms on one screen

There is, however, another reason for working through further example scenarios. My experience of teaching database design and development is that a lot of people have problems if the example used doesn't match their own context of use, even if, in logical terms, what you have to do is *exactly* the same.

Providing contextualisation to differently focussed groups over the years – students, unemployed people on Government training schemes, corporate administrators, small business owners, researchers, collectors and so on – seems to have been beneficial to each group. Even though we've now moved away from the need to understand relational design, I figured that the same approach would remain useful.

Basically, this section adds consolidation along with providing contextualisation to those in business or undertaking research by providing an opportunity to work though the TONTO Technique© again, this time using typical small business and research examples.

Small business scenario

Step 0. Are you already capturing data in some way?

STEP 0 CHECKLIST

1. *Look at any methods you currently use to capture your data.*
2. *Note data items where you enter the same data over and over.*

Let's assume that you aren't using any method to do what you want your database to do. From my own experience of running businesses, what people generally have is a drawer stuffed full of receipts and invoices that has to be pored through and reconciled come the end of the tax year. We've all been there.

This is a good way to illustrate that lacking a current method does not cause any difficulty whatsoever when using the TONTO Technique©.

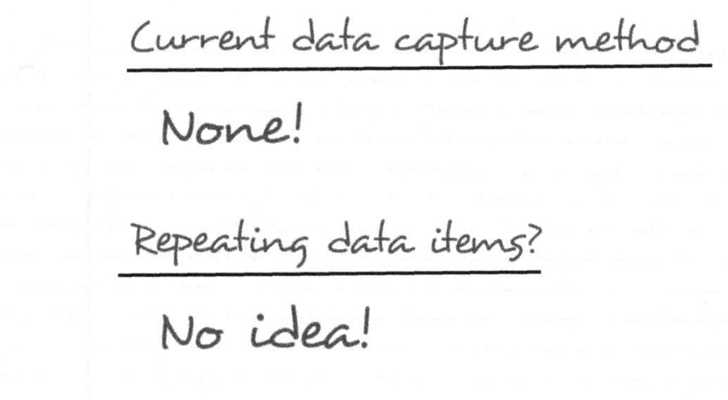

Figure 18. Often the starting point for relational database design.

Step 1. The scenario

STEP 1 CHECKLIST

1. Write down what you want your database to do for you.

I want to be able to keep track of expenditure for each project I undertake – that is, I want to know what I spend, the date, which company or person I'm paying, how much I'm spending on each transaction and how I pay – i.e. debit card, credit card, credit, cash etc. I need to be able to distinguish between services and actual items, which is something that I keep forgetting to keep track of. A prompt in the database will be very useful on this score. By the way, the items bought are hardly ever the same from project to project.

I also need to know which customer the project relates to so that I know who to bill for expenses to date. Customers pay for ongoing expenses during the life of the project and then pay the remainder of the originally agreed sum on project completion. Most customers are repeat customers.

It would be really nice if the database could print out the interim invoices for me to send too, or is that too much to ask? At the very least I need to know which items have already been invoiced for.

The only two irrelevant bits above are:

1. The prompt. This will just require the building of a pop–up message whenever someone forgets to enter that particular piece of data.
2. The printing out of invoices. This has to do with output, not input – though required outputs are good for hinting at some of the bits that you may have forgotten to otherwise write about. See below.

Invoicing is interesting – it isn't really just enough to have a tick box to see if something has already been invoiced. There looks to be the need for an invoice number so that the user can track on which invoice any one item was included. Now, you can have multiple items included on one invoice, so that means repeating the same piece of data. Yes, it looks as though invoice number will be a drop–down.

Step 2. Draw your data entry screen

STEP 2 CHECKLIST

1. *Draw your data entry screen(s), showing drop–downs and/or sub–forms.*
2. *Double check need for drop–downs with note made in Step 0.*

From the following data entry screen you can see that we have one drop–down in the main part of the form, plus a sub–form in which there are three drop–downs.

If you've had your thinking caps on, this should already tell you that your database will have six tables. It's all about drop–downs and sub–forms, remember; these tell you everything you need to know about the relational design.

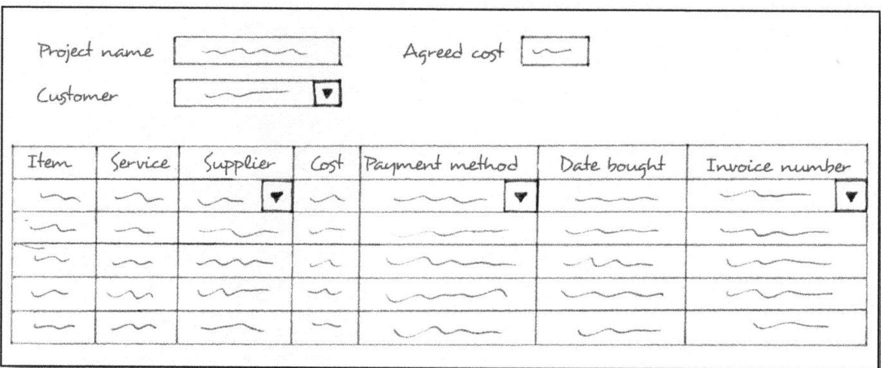

Figure 19. The required data entry screen. If you've been paying attention so far you should already have worked out that this design will equate to six tables.

In the above screen design, *Service* is a repeating field, but there can only ever be two options. It's either a service or it's not, so this will be a tick box. Where you only have two options, this will not become another table. Three items, however, is a different matter.

Step 3. The clever bit

STEP 3 CHECKLIST

1. *Ignore any sub–forms.*
2. *Draw tables for the main data entry screen and for each drop–down.*
3. *Write down all data entry fields for the main table.*
4. *Add the drop–down field(s) from main table to the drop–down table(s).*
5. *Add relationship(s) and add 1 and M at the appropriate ends.*

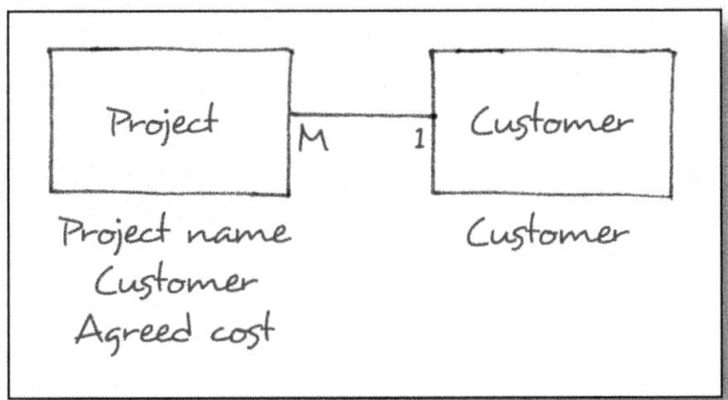

Figure 20. The main *Project* table and the drop–down *Customer* table showing the relationship.

We can already guess that some extra work will need to be done here because we have a name in a drop–down – although some of these customer names may be of organisations, some will almost certainly be of people, which needs two fields. Also, as already mentioned, where we have people or organisations, we generally also need to hold contact details.

However, we don't need to worry at this step. This is best left for later and is easily sorted out once you know what to do.

Step 4. The other clever bit

STEP 4 CHECKLIST

1. Draw tables for any sub–forms on your data entry screen.

2. Add relationship(s) between the sub–form table(s) and the main table and add 1 and M at the appropriate ends.

3. For any drop–downs in a sub–form, repeat Step 3 (make sure you do it between the right tables)

4. Join all the bits together.

This clever bit is very straightforward in this instance, so there is no need for expansion on this step. The three following Figures provide sufficient explanation.

We will, however, have some issues with supplier details for the same reason as with customer details in the previous step. Again, this can be ignored during this step and solved in the following step.

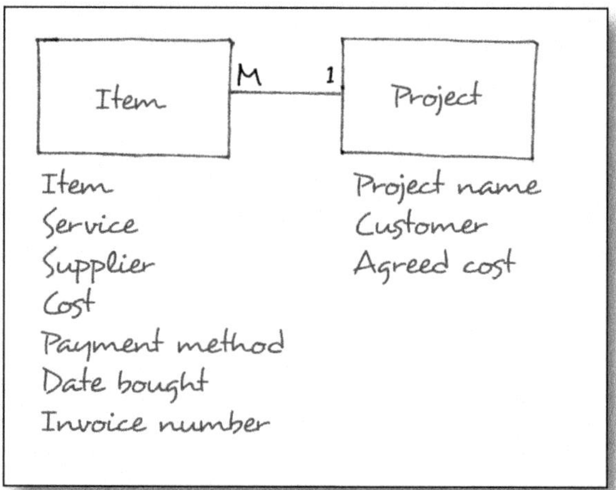

Figure 21. The main *Project* table and the sub–form *Item* table showing the relationship.

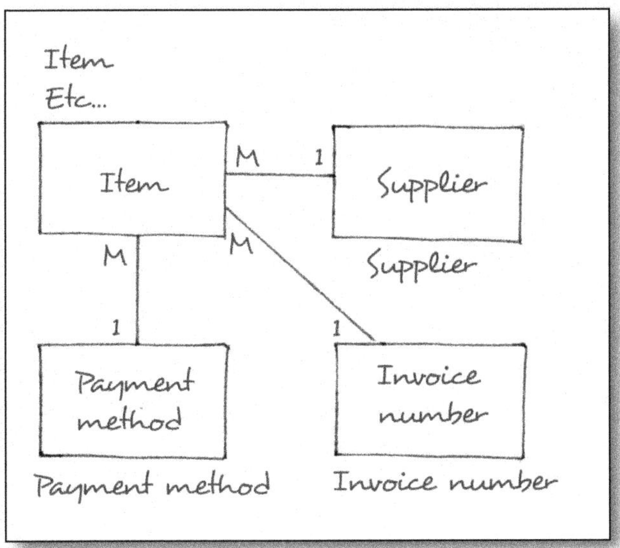

Figure 22. The sub–form table and the three drop–down tables showing relationships.

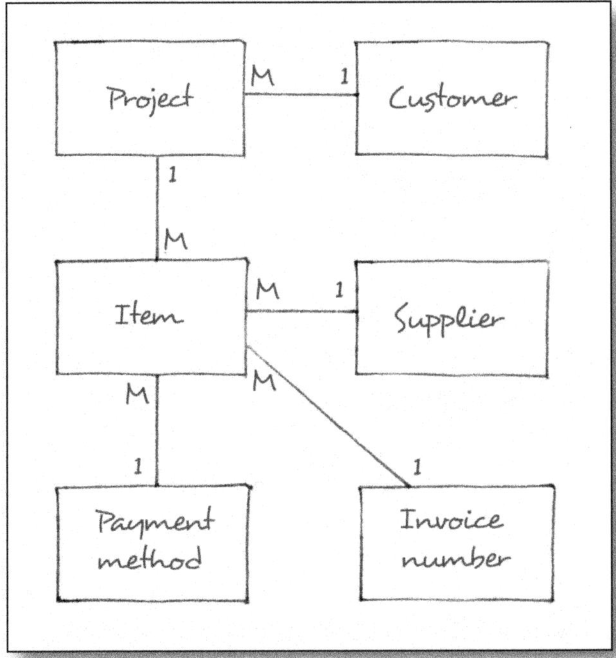

Figure 23. The whole relational database design.

Step 5. Tidy up the keys

STEP 5 CHECKLIST

1. Assign primary keys for each table.

2. Identify foreign keys where appropriate.

We have some issues with those drop–downs from which we want to choose the supplier or customer name. As already stated, names will always (or should always) be made up of at least two fields, one for first name and one for surname (if it's a business name rather than a person then it will just go in the second field). The trouble is that someone's name cannot be used as a primary key because lots of people have the same name – and you can only choose one field in a drop–down.

The way around this issue, as mentioned earlier, is to assign an auto number as the primary key for the customer and supplier tables. The foreign key will then be a number, formatted as long integer as per the rule for auto number foreign keys. (Relational database software, such as Microsoft Access 2013, can be set to let you see the name in the drop–down instead of the number.)

If you don't quite get it, don't worry, just follow what we do in this step and do the same whenever you hit the same situation.

Customer

As per the explanation directly above, we need to split the customer name into two fields. Without doing this there would have been no field that could uniquely identify every customer in the table; after doing this there still isn't! So add an auto number field and call it *Customer key*.

Following the rule for relationships, add *Customer key* (which is at the 1 end of the relationship) to the *Project* table (at the M end), **where it replaces the *Customer* field** that was added earlier.

Invoice number

No two invoice numbers (e.g. *XB1*, *LYGG2*, *CV3*, or whatever method of codification you choose) will be the same so you can make *Invoice number* the key field. We already have *Invoice number* in the *Item* table, where it is a foreign key.

Item

There is no field that can uniquely identify every item in the table – the Item field can't be used because, according to the scenario, there are occasionally duplicate items. Add an auto number field and call it *Item key*.

There is no relationship where *Item* appears at the 1 end, so *Item key* does not need to be put in any other table.

Payment method

No two payment methods (e.g. *Cheque*, *Cash*, *Credit*, etc.) will be the same so you can make *Payment method* the key field. We already have *Payment method* in the *Item* table, where it is a foreign key.

Project

There is no field that can uniquely identify every project in the table (it is *just* possible that more than one project can be given the same name although for different customers) so add an auto number field and call it *Project key*.

Following the rule for relationships, add *Project key* (which is at the 1 end of the relationship) to the *Customer* table (at the M end).

(Note: if no two projects could ever be given the same name then you could assign *Project name* as the key.)

Supplier

We need to split the supplier name into two fields and there is no field that can uniquely identify every supplier in the table. Add an auto number field and call it *Supplier key*.

Following the rule for relationships, add *Supplier key* (which is at the 1 end of the relationship) to the *Item* table (at the M end), **where it replaces the *Supplier* field**.

Step 6. Choose your data types and decide on size/format

STEP 6 CHECKLIST

1. *Decide on data type for every data entry field in every table.*
2. *Decide on field size and/or format for all fields.*

Table	Field name (key)	Data type	Size/format
Customer	Customer key (PK)	Auto Number	Default
	Customer name 1	Short Text	50
	Customer name 2	Short Text	50
Invoice number	Invoice number (PK)	Short Text	20
Item	Item key (PK)	Auto Number	Default
	Invoice number (FK)	Short Text	20
	Payment method (FK)	Short Text	30
	Project key (FK)	Number	Long Integer
	Supplier key (FK)	Number	Long Integer
	Item	Short Text	100
	Service	Yes/No	Default
	Cost	Currency	£
	Date bought	Date/Time	Long Date
Payment method	Payment method (PK)	Short Text	30
Project	Project key (PK)	Auto Number	Default
	Customer key (FK)	Number	Long Integer
	Project name	Short Text	100
	Agreed cost	Currency	£
Supplier	Supplier key (PK)	Auto Number	Default
	SupplierName1	Short Text	50
	SupplierName2	Short Text	50

Table 3. Business project database tables, fields and properties prior to tidying up.

As per the previous worked example, coming up with sizes for text fields is down to 'guestimation'. In the above example the designer was generous for the most part.

Step 7. Tidy up over a nice cup of tea

STEP 7 CHECKLIST

1. Add any further required fields to tables and deal with any new drop–downs or sub–forms as per Steps 3 and/or 4.

2. Remove calculations from tables.

3. Tidy up field and table names.

There are probably extra items that we want to record. As already mentioned, where you have a name, you probably want contact details as well. Also, knowing when an invoice was sent and payment status is probably useful information. We'll add fields for these to the relevant tables (and the ubiquitous comments fields).

Table	Field name (key)	Data type	Size/format
Customer	CustomerKey (PK)	Auto Number	Default
	CustomerName1	Short Text	50
	CustomerName2	Short Text	50
	Address1	Short Text	100
	Address2	Short Text	100
	Address3	Short Text	100
	Town	Short Text	100
	Postcode	Short Text	20
	Telephone	Short Text	100
	Email	Short Text	200
	Comments	Long Text	Default
InvoiceNumber	InvoiceNumber (PK)	Short Text	20
	DateSent	Date/Time	Long Date
	DatePaid	Date/Time	Long Date
	Comments	Long Text	Default
Item	ItemKey (PK)	Auto Number	Default
	InvoiceNumber (FK)	Short Text	20
	PaymentMethod (FK)	Short Text	30
	ProjectKey (FK)	Number	Long Integer
	SupplierKey (FK)	Number	Long Integer
	Item	Short Text	100
	Service	Yes/No	Default
	Cost	Currency	£
	DateBought	Date/Time	Long Date
	Comments	Long Text	Default

Table continued overleaf

Table	Field name (key)	Data type	Size/format
PaymentMethod	PaymentMethod (PK)	Short Text	30
	Comments	Long Text	Default
Project	ProjectKey (PK)	Auto Number	Default
	CustomerKey (FK)	Number	Long Integer
	ProjectName	Short Text	100
	AgreedCost	Currency	£
	Comments	Long Text	Default
Supplier	SupplierKey (PK)	Auto Number	Default
	SupplierName1	Short Text	50
	SupplierName2	Short Text	50
	Address1	Short Text	100
	Address2	Short Text	100
	Address3	Short Text	100
	Town	Short Text	100
	Postcode	Short Text	100
	Telephone	Short Text	100
	Email	Short Text	20
	Comments	Long Text	Default

Table 4. Business project database tables, fields and properties with database–friendly names.

Research scenario

Step 0. Are you already capturing data in some way?

STEP 0 CHECKLIST

1. Look at any methods you currently use to capture your data.

2. Note data items where you enter the same data over and over.

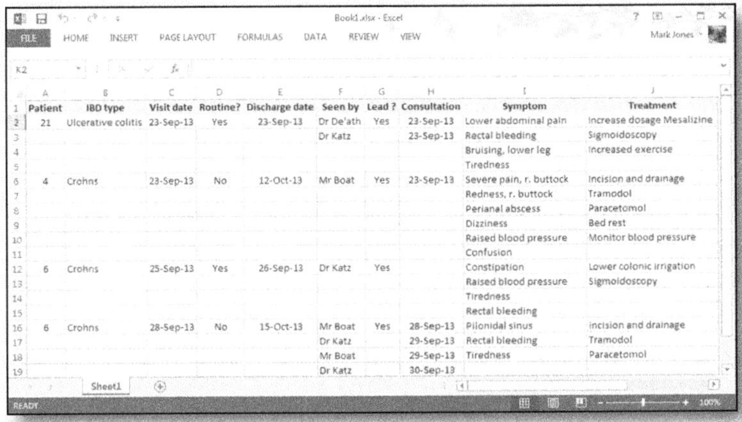

Patient	IBD type	Visit date	Routine?	Discharge date	Seen by	Lead ?	Consultation	Symptom	Treatment
21	Ulcerative colitis	23-Sep-13	Yes	23-Sep-13	Dr De'ath	Yes	23-Sep-13	Lower abdominal pain	Increase dosage Mesalizine
					Dr Katz		23-Sep-13	Rectal bleeding	Sigmoidoscopy
								Bruising, lower leg	Increased exercise
								Tiredness	
4	Crohns	23-Sep-13	No	12-Oct-13	Mr Boat	Yes	23-Sep-13	Severe pain, r. buttock	Incision and drainage
								Redness, r. buttock	Tramodol
								Perianal abscess	Paracetomol
								Dizziness	Bed rest
								Raised blood pressure	Monitor blood pressure
								Confusion	
6	Crohns	25-Sep-13	Yes	26-Sep-13	Dr Katz	Yes		Constipation	Lower colonic irrigation
								Raised blood pressure	Sigmoidoscopy
								Tiredness	
								Rectal bleeding	
6	Crohns	28-Sep-13	No	15-Oct-13	Mr Boat	Yes	28-Sep-13	Pilonidal sinus	Incision and drainage
					Dr Katz		29-Sep-13	Rectal bleeding	Tramodol
					Mr Boat		29-Sep-13	Tiredness	Paracetomol
					Dr Katz		30-Sep-13		

Figure 24. Only a very small section of a spread sheet with around another eight columns.

This is a very good example of why not to use spread sheets to store repeating data. In fact there should be more repeating data, but many cells have been left blank instead. All it's waiting for is a sorting disaster to mix all of this data up with no idea of to whom the majority of the data relates.

Another problem is that this makes it look as though symptoms have specific treatments (or not), which is not the case. These are both just lists of either symptom or treatment over the life of each visit – and dates for symptoms and treatments are conspicuous by their absence, so these can't be individually assigned.

Not all of the columns with repeating data will become tables. Those with dates will not, as already explained, become tables, so you can ignore these. Also, if a column has repeating data, but this data can only ever be one of two values (as in columns four and seven), then, again as already mentioned, these will be tick boxes instead.

The spread sheet provides a misleading idea of what data repeats and what does not. Sometimes it is better not to bother with step 0 even if you have been recording your data! If it doesn't help or just confuses you, then use it, but warily.

Step 1. The scenario

STEP 1 CHECKLIST

1. Write down what you want your database to do for you.

I'm researching into specific aspects of inflammatory bowel disease (IBD). There are eight possible types of IBD for the purposes of this research and each of the 100 patients that have agreed to partake in the project has already been diagnosed with one of these eight types. I need to know which type of IBD any given person has.

The main thrust of the research requires me to keep track of all routine (i.e. pre–arranged) or emergency visits made to the hospital by each patient. For each visit I need to record the date and time, which doctor the patient saw, if there were any symptoms recorded and what, if any, treatment was prescribed. I also need to record the discharge date if any patients were kept in hospital. That also means I have to be able to record the date of each individual consultation, treatment and so on, if not the same day as admission/appointment.

The main problem is that it is possible that the patient may be seen by more than one doctor in any given visit, though one will always be designated as 'lead' doctor so that final decision on treatment can be assigned to a single person throughout their stay. There is usually more than one symptom recorded on each visit and patients are often prescribed more than one treatment on any visit (i.e. not just medication, but perhaps dietary suggestions, exercise, etc.). The spread sheet's a real mess!

I want two data entry screens; the main one for visits and another one where I can add ongoing notes about individual patients.

I nearly forgot, patients are identified by codes instead of by names because of the Data Protection Act. Each patient has been given a number between 1 and 100. The database must not hold identifiable patient data.

The last paragraph means that we don't need two fields for the patient name. However, we'll still need two fields for doctor's names when we get to that point.

Step 2. Draw your data entry screen

STEP 2 CHECKLIST

1. Draw your data entry screen(s), showing drop–downs and/or sub–forms.

2. Double check need for drop–downs with note made in Step 0.

In this instance two data entry screens have been stipulated, so you can see how to deal with this. If even more screens were required, you would do exactly the same as here, one more time for each screen required.

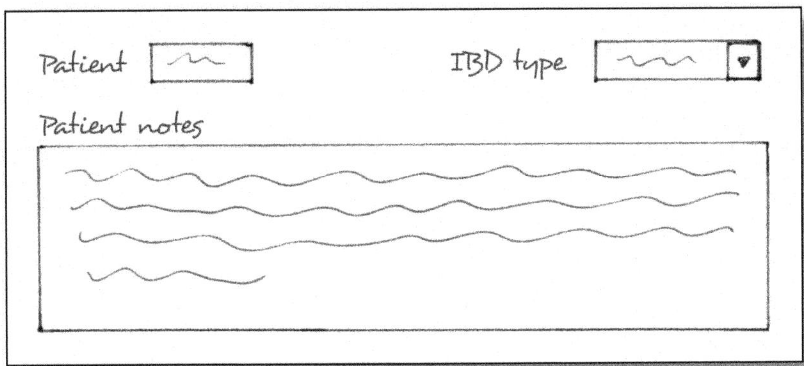

Figure 25. The data entry screen for entering patient details..

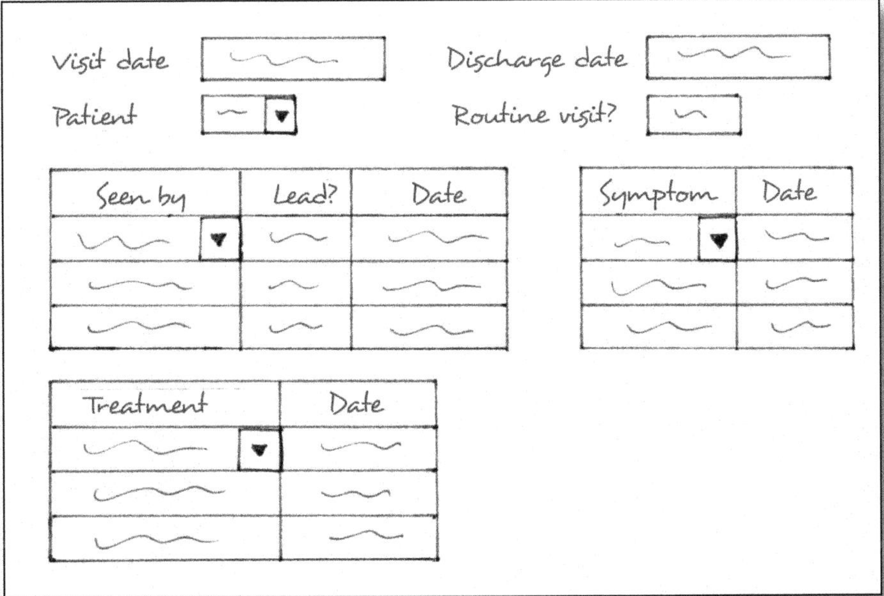

Figure 26. The main data entry screen, this for entering visit details.

Step 3. The clever bit

STEP 3 CHECKLIST

1. *Ignore any sub–forms.*
2. *Draw tables for the main data entry screen and for each drop–down.*
3. *Write down all data entry fields for the main table.*
4. *Add the drop–down field(s) from main table to the drop–down table(s).*
5. *Add relationship(s) and add 1 and M at the appropriate ends.*

There will be nine tables by the look of things. Not that it matters how many tables there are. The process is exactly the same each time. If there are more drop–downs or sub–forms it just means that it will take a bit longer to get through this and the following step.

However, two data entry screens brings a little more more complexity, so the best way to deal with complexity, as always, is a little at a time. The first clever bit is relatively easy to do. The only difference is that because there are two data entry screens, we have to do it twice. The other clever bit will be a bit harder, but only because there's more to do.

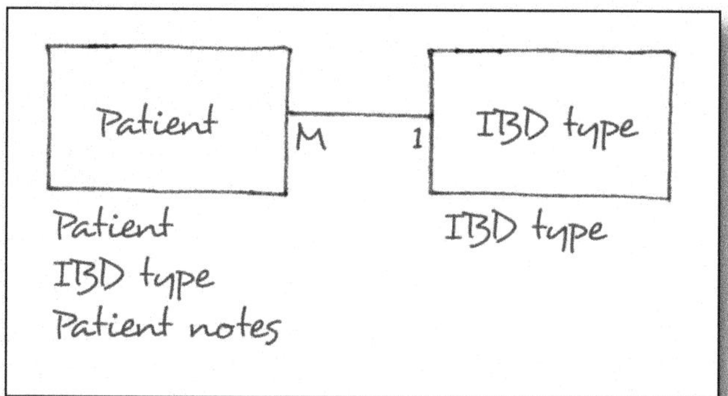

Figure 27. The main *Patient* table (from the first data entry screen) and the drop–down *IBD type* table showing the relationship.

The only potentially confusing part is that the *Patient* table is identified from both data entry screens (Figures 27 and 28). As long as you cope with the concept that this is the same table viewed from two screens rather than being two different tables, then there should be no problems.

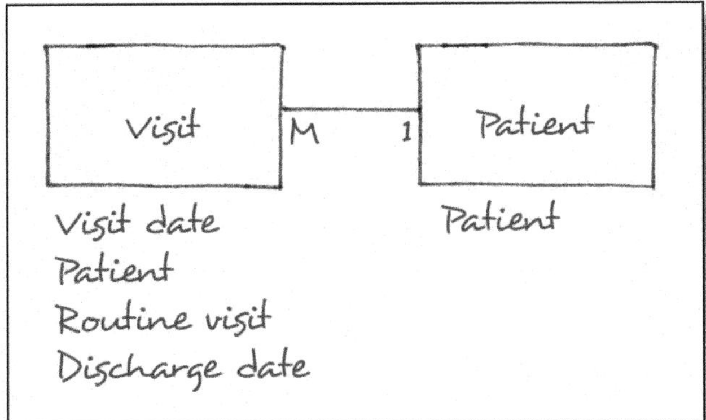

Figure 28. The main *Visit* table (from the second data entry screen) and the drop–down *Patient* table showing the relationship.

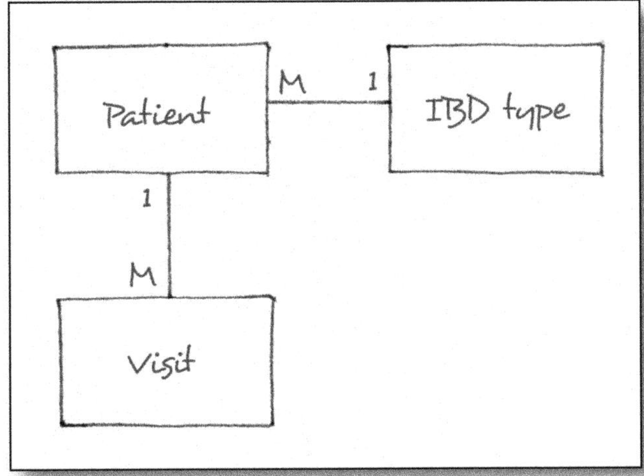

Figure 29. The three tables so far showing the relationships. Note that although both data entry screens have identified a *Patient* table, these are, of course, the same table, just seen from different screens.

Step 4. The other clever bit

STEP 4 CHECKLIST

1. Draw tables for any sub–forms on your data entry screen.

2. Add relationship(s) between the sub–form table(s) and the main table and add 1 and M at the appropriate ends.

3. For any drop–downs in a sub–form, repeat Step 3 (make sure you do it between the right tables)

4. Join all the bits together.

If both data entry screens had included sub–forms, then we'd have to do this part for each sub–form on each screen. As it is, the first screen has no sub–form so we can ignore it. On the other hand, just to make up, the second screen has three sub–forms, each of which has a drop–down.

Working out that you have four tables to begin with is easy – that's one for the main form and one each for the sub–forms. However, each sub–form has one drop–down, so we can see that there will be another three tables as well.

This is easy to deal with, providing you deal with one sub–form at a time. So the suggestion is to work through the *Seen by* sub–form first. Once you've finished with that, then move on to the *Treatment* sub–form and so on.

By doing it in stages it's just like a simple jig–saw puzzle, in that where each part goes is easy to work out. If you try to do the whole thing at once it can get a bit overwhelming. Look at the following figures to see how to approach this task.

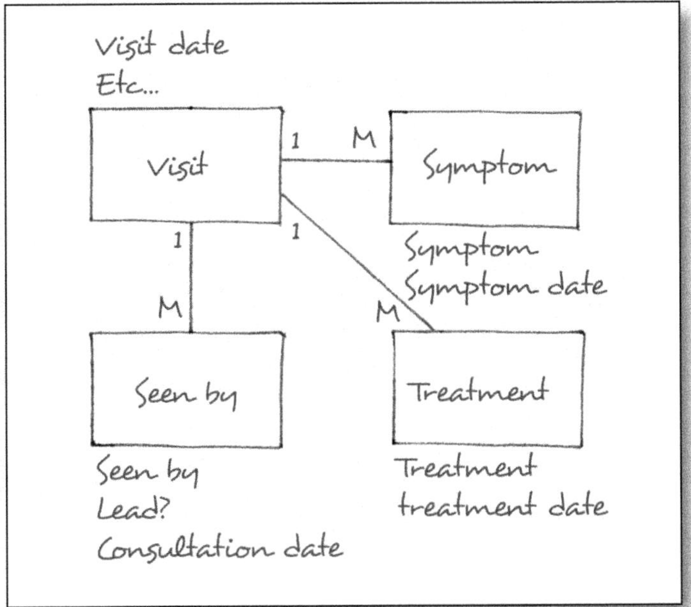

Figure 30. The main *Visit* table and the three sub–form tables showing relationships

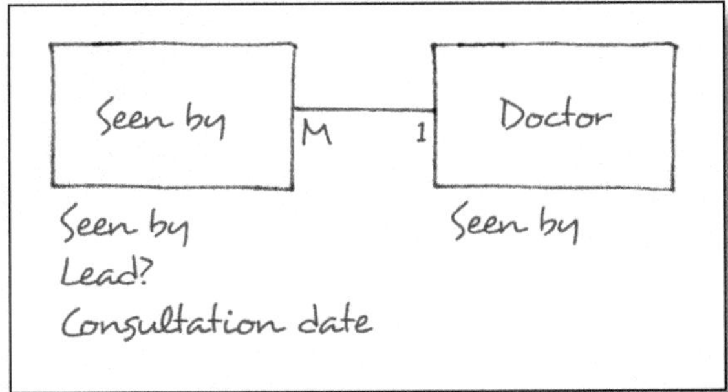

Figure 31. The *Seen by* (sub–form) table and the drop–down *Doctor* table showing the relationship.

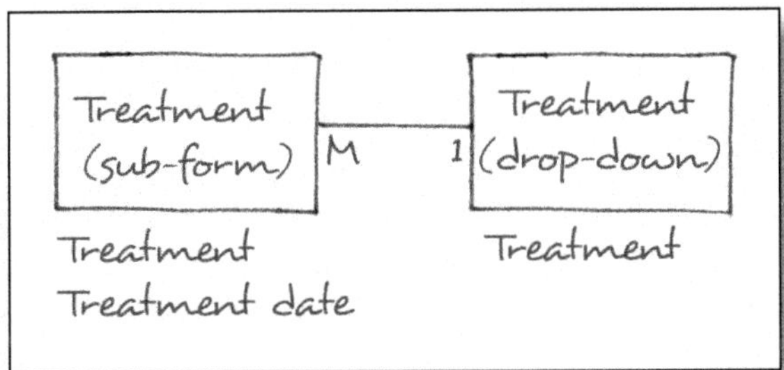

Figure 32. The *Treatment* (sub–form) table and the *Treatment drop–down* table showing the relationship.

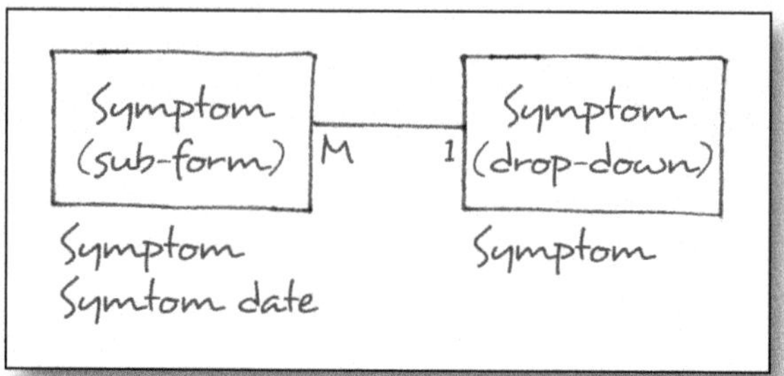

Figure 33. The *Symptom* (sub–form) table and the *Symptom drop–down* table showing the relationship.

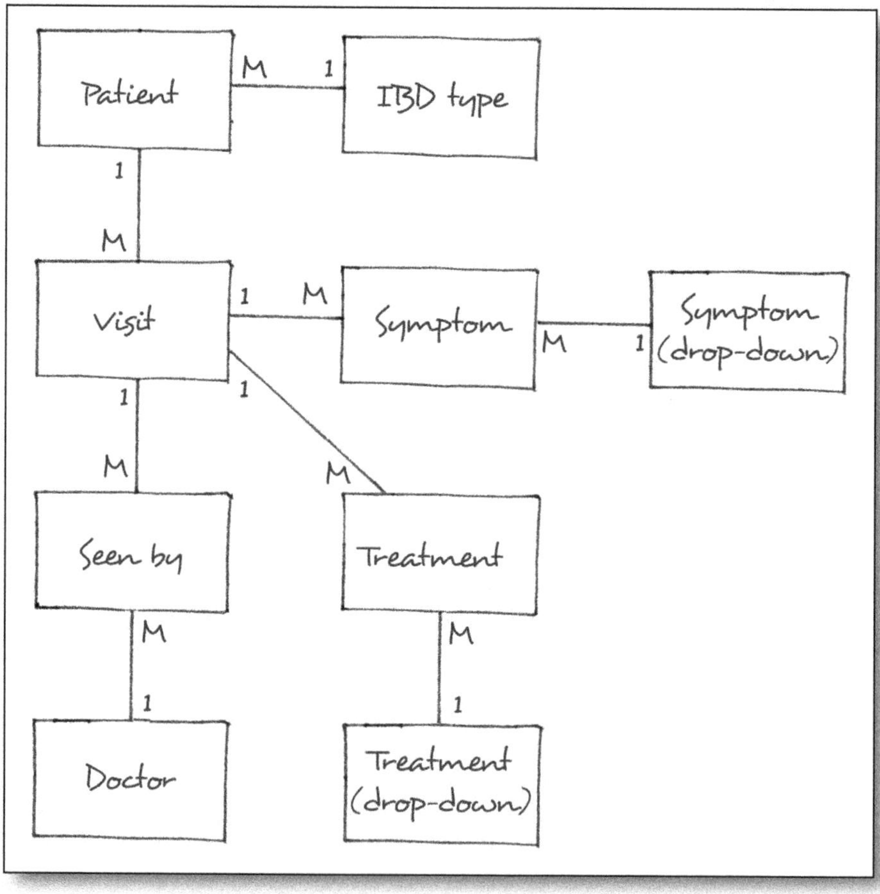

Figure 34. A perfect relational design showing all the parts joined together. However, this could have been a lot more complicated if the project had required the tying of every treatment to a specific symptom or set of symptoms. As it was, the project didn't require this. Instead, each visit required a post–visit write up to tie all the ends together, which prompted the researcher to realise that she'd forgotten to add a comments field to the data entry screen design. This is remedied in the last step.

Step 5. Tidy up the keys

STEP 5 CHECKLIST

1. Assign primary keys for each table.

2. Identify foreign keys where appropriate.

We have the same issue for the doctor drop–down as in the previous example with customer and supplier. The solution here is exactly the same.

The only confusing thing is that we have some similar sounding table names. This often can't be helped but, again, do things one at a time to keep it simple.

Doctor

As per the explanation above, we need to split the doctor name (the current *Seen by* field) into two fields. There is no field that can uniquely identify every doctor in the table so add an auto number field and call it *Doctor key*. Whilst we're at it, we might as well give the two fields for doctors' names sensible names, such as *Doctor name 1* and *Doctor name 2* rather than using the original *Seen by* name.

Following the rule for keys, add *Doctor key* (from the 1 end of the relationship) to the *Seen by* table (at the M end), **where it replaces the *Seen by* field**.

IBD type

No two IBD types are the same so make *IBD type* the key field. We already have *IBD type* in the *Patient* table, where it is a foreign key.

Patient

No two patients will be the same – because they have been assigned code numbers instead of using names – so make *Patient* the key field. We already have *Patient* in the *Visit* table, where it is a foreign key.

Seen by

There is no field that can uniquely identify every record in the table (one or more patients can see the same doctor over and over again) so add an auto number field and call it *Seen by key*.

There is no relationship where *Seen by* appears at the 1 end, so *Seen by key* does not need to be put in any other table.

Symptom

There is no field that can uniquely identify every record in the table (one or more patient visit can throw up – no pun intended – the same symptom over and over again) so add an auto number field and call it *Symptom key*.

There is no relationship where *Symptom* appears at the 1 end, so *Symptom key* does not need to be put in any other table.

Symptom drop-down table

No two symptoms in the drop–down (e.g. *Weight loss*, *Vomiting*, etc.) will be the same so make *Symptom* the key field. We already have *Sympton* in the *Symptom* table, where it is a foreign key.

Treatment

There is no field that can uniquely identify every record in the table (one or more patient visit can result in the same treatment). Add an auto number field and call it *Treatment key*.

There is no relationship where *Treatment* appears at the 1 end, so *Treatment key* does not need to be put in any other table.

Treatment drop-down table

No two treatments in the drop–down (e.g. *Large bowel resection*, *Mesalazine*, *Exercise*, etc.) will be the same so make *Treatment* the key field. We already have *Treatment* in the *Treatment* table, where it is a foreign key.

Visit

There is no field that can uniquely identify every patient's visit in the table – it is possible that two patients can have visits on the same date, so date won't do – so add an auto number field and call it *Visit key*.

Following the rule for relationships, add *Visit key* (which is at the 1 end of three separate relationships) to the *Treatment*, *Doctor* and *Symptom* tables (all of which are at the M end of their respective relationships).

Step 6. Choose your data types and decide on size/format

STEP 6 CHECKLIST

1. *Decide on data type for every data entry field in every table.*
2. *Decide on field size and/or format for all fields.*

Table	Field name (key)	Data type	Size/format
Doctor	Doctor key (PK)	Auto Number	Default
	Doctor name 1	Short Text	50
	Doctor name 2	Short Text	50
IBD type	IBD type (PK)	Short Text	40
Patient	Patient (PK)	Short Text	10
	IBD type (FK)	Short Text	40
	Patient notes	Long Text	Default
Seen by	Seen by key (PK)	Auto Number	Default
	Doctor key (FK)	Number	Long Integer
	Visit key (FK)	Number	Long Integer
	Lead	Yes/No	Default
	Consultation date	Date/Time	Long date
Symptom (sub-form)	Symptom key (PK)	Auto Number	Default
	Symptom (FK)	Short Text	100
	Visit key (FK)	Number	Long Integer
	Symptom date	Date/Time	Long date
Symptom (drop-down)	Symptom (PK)	Short Text	100
Treatment (sub-form)	Treatment key (PK)	Auto Number	Default
	Treatment (FK)	Short Text	100
	Visit key (FK)	Number	Long Integer
	Treatment date	Date/Time	Long date
Treatment (drop-down)	Treatment (PK)	Short Text	100
Visit	Visit key (PK)	Auto Number	Default
	Patient (FK)	Short Text	10
	Routine	Yes/No	Default
	Visit date	Date/Time	Long Date
	Discharge date	Date/Time	Long Date

Table 5. IBD research project database tables, fields and properties prior to tidying up.

Step 7. Tidy up over a nice cup of tea

STEP 7 CHECKLIST

1. Add any further required fields to tables and deal with any new drop–downs or sub–forms as per Steps 3 and/or 4.

2. Remove calculations from tables.

3. Tidy up field and table names.

Apart from adding comments fields to each table (*Patient* already has a long text field for adding patient notes but there's nothing to stop you adding a comments field as well) there's very little to add. You might want to add fields for *Salutation* (e.g. Dr, Mr, etc.) and *Doctor type* (e.g. Registar, Consultant, etc.) to the table holding doctors' names. Both of these, of course would mean duplicated data and so two further tables to add to your design. I haven't bothered here because these details were considered as 'nice–to–know' rather than 'must– know' and this data was just added to the comments field. If this data had been required for structured output in datasets for analysis, then that would be a different matter.

One other thing was that, although not mentioned in the scenario, it later became obvious that recording patients' gender and age would be very useful for identifying trends. Therefore two further fields were added to the *Patient* table.

The main problem is that we have tables with similar names, so we need to think of a way to name these so that there is no confusion when we come to using the database once built. In database terms, any table that feeds a drop–down is termed a *look–up* table, so we can name those tables with similar names as, for example, *Treatment* and *TreatmentLookUp* to make it obvious which is which.

The only other thing to do is to look at the table names and see if you can find more sensible names for them – often the hardest part of database design is coming up with sensible names for things. All of these are fairly self–evident names – in that the name of the table tells you pretty much what will go in each. The only one I don't really like is the *SeenBy* table. I'm going to change it to *Consultation* – after all, we've already called the date field in that table *Consultation date* so as to distinguish it from the various other date fields in other tables.

So the *SeenBy* table becomes *Consultation* and the field *SeenByKey* can be renamed as *ConsultationKey*. Remember that if you rename a primary key field then you will need to also rename it in any tables where it appears as a foreign key. In this instance the *SeenByKey* doesn't live in any other tables so we don't have to worry about it.

Table	Field name (key)	Data type	Size/format
Consultation	ConsultationKey (PK)	Auto Number	Default
	DoctorKey (FK)	Number	Long Integer
	VisitKey (FK)	Number	Long Integer
	Lead	Yes/No	Default
	ConsultationDate	Date/Time	Long Date
	Comments	Long Text	Default
Doctor	DoctorKey (PK)	Auto Number	Default
	DoctorName1	Short Text	50
	DoctorName2	Short Text	50
	Comments	Long Text	Default
IBDType	IBDType (PK)	Short Text	40
	Comments	Long Text	Default
Patient	Patient (PK)	Short Text	10
	IBDType (FK)	Short Text	40
	DateOfBirth	Date/Time	Long Date
	Female	Yes/No	Default
	PatientNotes	Long Text	Default
Symptom	SymptomKey (PK)	Auto Number	Default
	Symptom (FK)	Text	100
	VisitKey (FK)	Number	Long Integer
	SymptomDate	Date/Time	Long Date
	Comments	Long Text	Default
SymptomLookUp	Symptom (PK)	Short Text	100
	Comments	Long Text	Default
Treatment	TreatmentKey (PK)	Auto Number	Default
	Treatment (FK)	Short Text	100
	VisitKey (FK)	Number	Long Integer
	TreatmentDate	Date/Time	Long Date
	Comments	Long Text	Default
TreatmentLookUp	Treatment (PK)	Short Text	100
	Comments	Long Text	Default
Visit	VisitKey (PK)	Auto Number	Default
	Patient (FK)	Short Text	10
	Routine	Yes/No	Default
	VisitDate	Date/Time	Long Date
	DischargeDate	Date/Time	Long Date
	Comments	Long Text	Default

Table 6. IBD research project database tables, fields and properties with database–friendly names.

Building Relational Databases Made Easy
M. Clinton Jones

ISBN: 978-1-909953-56-7
RRP: £15.99
Published by Diogenes Academic Press
www.bristol-folk.co.uk

So now that you've got your relational design, you must be eager to get started on building your database. Cue *Building Relational Databases Made Easy*.

This book starts where *Database Design Made Easy* leaves off and takes the same informal, though tip–packed, approach to guide you through how to build, using the current version of Microsoft Access, the databases designed in this current book.

Many database development books do little more than take you through the functionality and features available in whichever software package it is that they describe. The difference with this book is that, using the examples from *Database Design Made Easy*, it shows you what to do to turn *any* paper–based relational database design into a working database. Whether your design includes two tables or two hundred, this book sets you on the right path.

It does this by concentrating on the *building blocks* required to build a database, rather than focussing on any particular software features. That said, once the database is built, the book suggests some 'bells and whistles' that will make using your database a bit easier.

Like *Database Design Made Easy*, this book is also printed on demand so as to save trees and help to keep remainders shops free from too much clutter. Printing on demand means that the book is only manufactured at the point at which you buy it. So as to be yet more environmentally friendly, the author suggests using recycled pixels to build your database, though we're fairly convinced that this is an attempt at a joke. Just not a very funny one.

Space for designing your own database

Space for designing your own database

Space for designing your own database

Space for designing your own database

Space for designing your own database

Space for designing your own database

www.ingramcontent.com/pod-product-compliance
Ingram Content Group UK Ltd.
Pitfield, Milton Keynes, MK11 3LW, UK
UKHW021941200726
13856UKWH00005B/1238